S0-BRM-295

The Missing Piece

Compiled by

KATE GARDNER

The Missing Piece: A Transformational Journey

Copyright © 2013, Kate Gardner – Empowering Coaching 4 Women
www.empoweringcoaching4women.com

All rights reserved worldwide.

No part of this book may be used or reproduced in any manner without written permission. This publication is protected under the US Copyright Act of 1976 and all other applicable international, federal, state and local laws, and all rights are reserved, including resale rights.

Coaching and Success
c/o Marketing for Coach, Ltd
Second Floor
6th London Street
W2 1HR London (UK)

www.coachingandsuccess.com
info@coachingandsuccess.com

ISBN: 978-0-9575561-7-1

Published in UK, Europe, US and Canada

Book Cover: Csernik Előd

Inside Layout: Csernik Előd

Table of Contents

Disclaimer

Every word in this book is based on the co- authors' personal experiences. The results they have achieved using the tips included in their chapters are not scientifically proven. The results are based on what was achieved when the authors incorporated these strategies into their lives.

I have made every reasonable attempt for all chapters to not include names of third parties and instead use false names. I assume no responsibility for the authors sharing their private experiences with the world. The information provided within these pages is solely your responsibility of how you incorporate it into your own life.

Nothing in this book is a quick fix promise or in any way a means to name and shame people. It is solely a platform for the authors and myself to share our experiences and spread a light upon the world and give tips and advice to those who choose to take it and place it within their lives.

Nothing in this book is intended to replace any medical or psychological advice. Each person's results may vary.

In Loving Memory

"We all have people within our lives that mean the world to us and have inspired and impacted our lives in some way. Through our eyes we see them as strong invincible people who we think will be around forever. Only the sad fact is that they are not invincible. Without us expecting it, they leave us to join god's side, which leaves you with a great big hole of emptiness they once filled. Only they didn't leave you with nothing! In fact they left you with their inspiration for a reason, and that was so you could take that inspiration and shine it upon the world."

In Loving Memory of
William & Sheila Whiteoak, my amazing grandparents

and

Nealey Jo Nicholson, whose 30 short years on earth touched so many hearts, including mine.

Thank You

I just had to begin this book first by thanking those who made it possible for me to be where I am today. This book would not even be possible if not for these amazing people within my life, and they need to be told how special they are to me.

I would first like to give a huge thank you to my partner Matthew. He is the most supportive partner in the world. He is not just my partner; he is my best friend, soul mate and cheerleader all rolled into one. Life without him would be very dull and boring. Even though he drives me crazy sometimes with his daft sense of humor, I love him to pieces and I am so looking forward to becoming his wife next year when we marry.

A special huge thank you to my two amazing children, Emily and Jordan. Every day I do what I do because of these two incredible human beings. I am hugely proud of you both for growing into the amazing, respectable, young people that you are today. You are my world and I love you very much.

A huge thank you to my amazing business partners, friends, and soul sisters, Christine Marmoy and Kim B. Smith. The day these ladies came into my life is the day my life, business and everything else changed. Not only did I have these two amazing women come into my life, but I also had coaches, accountability partners and personal butt kickers all at the same time. They saw in me what I could not yet identify, and they both work with me daily to pull my greatness out of me.

I would also like to thank my amazing team of The Freedom & Empowerment Campaign and wonderful Ambassadors who have stood beside my mission all the way, and also my incredible coaches who transformed my mindset and shaped who I am now, including Vasavi Kumar who kindly wrote the foreword of this book for me.

Last but not least, my biggest heartfelt thank you goes to Jack Canfield. He was my first ever life coach, and he picked me up from my concrete bottom and laid the foundations for who I am today. This book is the result of your "Rule of Five," Jack, so thank you!

Foreword

If you are someone who is experiencing some form of struggle in life, or perhaps you work with people who day in and day out question the meaning of their self-worth and value because of the things they have tolerated in life, this book is for you. As Kate's Life coach, it was inevitable that she would ask me to write the foreword for her book, undoubtedly given my own thriver story. I believe that regardless of one's path, no matter how bumpy, how obstacle-ridden, how treacherous and windy, everyone has the ability to bounce back and thrive tenfold.

The Missing Piece is a result of Kate's implementation of the "Rule of Five"- a tool that was taught to her by her very first mentor, Jack Canfield. It is no mistake that in the midst of Kate's chaos, while she was unpacking her boxes she found the book *The Secret* by Rhonda Byrne buried at the bottom of her boxes. This "Secret," also known as the Law of Attraction, would then lead her to her very first mentor Jack Canfield, who would then teach her the Rule of Five.

Now, what is this Rule of Five you may be wondering? Well, simply stated, when you practice the Rule of Five, you complete five goals per day to reach the big picture you have in your mind. Little did Kate know that by incorporating the Rule of Five into her life, she would be able to overcome the trauma associated with her domestic violence and her daughter's rape.

Kate is the very definition of a thriver. A brief glimpse into her book will allow any reader into the darkest moments in her life. It's evident that Kate is a living example of what it truly means to go from barely surviving, to fully thriving. To thrive should not be underrated.

It took courage for Kate to move past tolerating what is, to stand for what she truly believed in. It took trust and surrender to allow herself to share her story openly for the world to experience. That is exactly what Kate did and the others here in this book. She created a platform for other amazing people to share their stories, so as to inspire and touch so many readers, who in these kind of situations, can possibly have a glimmer of hope that maybe they too can find the missing piece in their lives.

While nobody says it outright, the fact of the matter remains the same – that victims of domestic violence are viewed as shameful and unacceptable. The taboo that women who stay in abusive relationships are weak and crazy is a stigma that women who live in abusive relationships have to bear every single day of their lives. But of course, like many other "socially inappropriate" topics, domestic violence is not one that is talked about out loud and in public. While the immediate costs of domestic violence are somewhat obvious, from destroying careers, to ruining relationships, to damaging one's self image and worth, the costs associated with NOT speaking of this prevalent issue are far greater – in essence, a quiet acceptance of violence and emotional abuse. And Kate overcame this to become who she is today!

It is an honor and privilege to have worked with Kate, to watch her thrive in all aspects of her life and to help others do the same. I have no doubt in my mind that this book will be a catalyst of inspiration for all the readers that are able to get their hands on this book, a true testament to what it means to make a shift and find that missing piece so that they can move forward fast.

By Vasavi Kumar
International Best Selling Author/
Speaker & Celebrity Life Coach
www.vasavikumar.com

Introduction

I will never forget the day that the idea for *The Missing Piece* came to me. I jumped out of bed one morning in May 2013, and the idea hit me like a thunderbolt. I had this overwhelming feeling to put this project together and to shine the knowledge of others onto the world.

Now this was huge for me! I felt sick with nerves.

At the time I was involved in Christine Marmoy's *Hot Mama in (High) Heels* project. I approached her and told her of my idea about a three book project, which at the beginning I thought she would reply with, "you are crazy!"

But Christine supported me 1000% and thought it was a great idea. So I set out on my journey to find amazing women all around the world with incredible stories. Those who have experienced real hardships and have come out on the other side; those who have completely transformed themselves to become who they are today. At first I thought I had bitten off more than I could chew with this project. I thought I would never find enough women to fill a book. I thought I must be crazy thinking I could ever pay this off.

I put the project out into the world and then these amazing women came forward. One by one, they came with truly amazing stories, some of which made me speechless. I was in complete awe of what these women had experienced and the wonderful people that they had transformed into. Reading their stories made no room for excuses in my own life.

During the middle of the project was a hard time for me. I was sent the greatest test of all to see if, in spite of everything, I could keep this project going. I received a message informing me that one of my close friends had died. I went into shock and could not quite grasp what I was hearing.

Nealey Jo Nicholson passed away on July 7, 2013, at the very young age of 30. In her 30 short years on this planet she touched many hearts and made everyone in her presence laugh. She had a great sense of humor and there was never a dull moment in the room with her around.

Nealey was always so proud of me for my work and always told me so when I was with her. For me this was huge, because I had never received much praise from people in my life; she lit me up when she praised my writing.

I sat at my desk the morning after she had passed away crying and staring at my computer screen. I felt so numb and shocked – like I couldn't carry on. Suddenly, the hairs on the back of my neck stood on end. Then goose bumps appeared all over my arms, and I relived all the times in my head that Nealey had praised my work.

This made me spring into action and continue my search for fascinating people with transformational stories. Despite losing my voice through grief I continued to work hard on the project.

The Missing Piece: A Transformational Journey shares experiences that will shock you, make you speechless and inspire you. When I read the stories within this book, I was completely in awe and the tears flowed down my face.

I admire the strength of these women, and what they have had to face and overcome to be who they are today. Not many things leave me speechless in life, but this book sure did!

The most admiring thing about these authors is that they have not only shared their experiences with you, but they leave you with something that you can incorporate into your life to move you forward. They have left you with a complete guide on how to keep going after difficult and life changing experiences. They didn't want to just give you a chapter of what they had been through; they wanted to leave something at the end to help you too. The authors have also left their contact details and links to their websites so that you can connect with them on a personal level after you have read their stories.

This book is truly from all our hearts, and it's a way to give you pieces of hope that you need to shine a ray of light on you when you feel low. I never want you to feel like anything is impossible, because trust me, all of us in this book are living proof that it is possible to put your life back together after such trying times.

If you only take one thing away from this book then please take this:

This project all started from an idea – an idea that came from a child who came from a poor background, who was bullied most of her life, and was groomed for failure, which then set the foundations for one abusive relationship after another in her adulthood, until it nearly cost her life through having a stroke at the age of 31 years old. She was put down constantly by people and was told she would never amount to anything or become anyone and was left with zero confidence and frozen in fear (so much so that she feared making phone calls). She lost five people in five years who were near and dear to her. Then she had to watch the cycle of abuse relive itself within her 14-year-old child when she became a victim of dating abuse and was raped.

But despite all that, she conquered her fears, her drinking and drug problems and her demons with unstoppable strength so that she could bring you this project today.

You now have the power of this book within your hands, which includes the missing pieces you have been searching for.

Please use it and thrive with it. Then contact the authors and myself because we want to hear your success stories.

Here's to your success!

Kate Gardner
International Best Selling Author/Empowerment Coach
Video Creative Director & Founder of the Freedom &
Empowerment Campaign

11

Kate Gardner

Kate Gardner is an International Best Selling Author/Empowerment Coach & Video Creative Director who works closely with International Best Selling Authors and business owners to help them launch their books and products with video. Kate is also an empowerment coach who helps women become empowered and find their purpose. Kate is also the compiler of this amazing book project and the founder of the global campaign, The Freedom & Empowerment Campaign.

If you are a woman who longs to feel empowered and to be able to push past your fears and take your world to a whole new level, then visit Kate's website.

www.empoweringcoaching4women.com

www.successfulvideo.com

www.the-missing-piece.com

www.freedomandempowerment.com

✉ **Kate@empoweringcoaching4women.com**

f **facebook.com/KIT1979**

🐦 **twitter.com/kategardner1979**

CHAPTER 1

THE RULE OF FIVE

By Kate Gardner

The Rule of Five was taught to me by my first ever life coach Jack Canfield. He taught me to take five small steps a day and these five small steps would then take me closer to my huge goals of where I wanted to be.

You see, 18 months ago I was not an International Best Selling Author/ Empowerment Coach to Women and Video Creative Director who works everyday with International Best Selling Authors. I was not the founder of a global domestic violence campaign called The Freedom & Empowerment Campaign, which is known within 44 countries and comprises a team of 20 people across 7 countries – a team that includes Ambassadors who are #1 Best Selling Authors – and I was not a compiler of this amazing book!

In fact, I was the complete opposite. 18 months ago I was sitting on the corner of my bed staring at the wall with my heart ripped to shreds.

Why?

Because I was experiencing heartbreak and experiencing a pain that I would never wish on any mother who has a daughter. I had just come home that evening from a rape centre with my daughter who was 14 years old at the time. A month prior to this, she had been raped by a 17-year-old boy. The day I found out about this I was out in my local town doing my shopping and rushing around doing a million jobs at once like all mums do.

My mobile started to ring, and I searched frantically in my handbag. Eventually I found it and answered. My daughter's voice was on the other end of the line. She was really upset, and I couldn't string two words together of what she was saying.

Through Emily's sobs my brain picked up only five words: "Mum, I have been raped." The shock that hit me forced me to hold on to the wall in front of me. My knees felt like they were going to give way. I tried everything to concentrate on not having an anxiety attack, as the last anxiety attack I had caused a stroke, which left me paralyzed down my right side for two months afterward. It took all my mental strength and will to prevent that from happening again.

I told Emily I would be with her as soon as possible and hung up the phone. I sat down on a bench in the middle of town my mind spinning, and tried to clear the fog from my mind. My main priority right now was getting to my daughter, so I had no time for anxiety!

Emily was extremely brave and reported her attacker to the police. The strength in this girl astounded me! She was so determined to bring her attacker to justice, and as her mother I was so proud.

The next 6 months of Emily's life were a living hell. She would wake up screaming in the middle of the night, walk around the house at 3, 4 or 5 am in the morning. She wouldn't eat and would scream at everyone for every little thing.

I painted on the brave face that every parent does with their child. I lay with Emily every night for 6 months till she fell asleep in my arms. As soon as her eyes closed and the pain eased off her face, my tears would fall.

My pain inside was raw. Not only did it cut me deep to see my child experience so much pain, but I also had to mourn the loss of the daughter I had before. Emily was no longer the girl who only worried about a hair not being completely straight on her head, or what color eye shadow would go with her outfit.

She was now a girl whose innocence was robbed and the weight of the world on her shoulders. We had lost the old Emily forever.

During the time up to the court trial, Emily's attacker kept stalking her. He would wait outside the school gates for her with his friends and make her life more unbearable. This got so bad that we had to have Emily police escorted inside the school gates at the beginning and end of each school day.

Then, to add insult to injury, Emily's attacker moved into a house on the same road as us! This sent Emily's emotions completely overboard, and she had an emotional breakdown. She began suffering from anxiety and would not leave the house to go to school. The few times she did go were short lived and resulted in me receiving a phone call from the headmaster an hour later saying that Emily had broken down in class and the teachers couldn't calm her.

The only way forward for us all was to place Emily into therapy. She started visiting the school's counselor once a week, and she also visited the crisis rape centre that was run by plain-clothes police officers and psychologists to support rape victims before their trials.

On one particular visit to the rape centre we had to wait in the waiting room. The memory that I hold in my mind from that day has stayed with me, and it is the fuel that led me to set up a global domestic violence campaign.

While Emily and I were waiting for our turn to see the officer dealing with Emily's case, there was a woman who had just come out of one of the interview rooms; this lady was standing outside the window I was looking out of. The lady stood waiting near the officer's car to be taken home because she feared going outside alone.

The woman stood with her head and back hunched over and staring at the floor; her eyes were all red and puffy from where she was crying. She held a handkerchief in her hands, and she was twisting it tighter and tighter. You could see how sore it was making her fingers from the twisting. The realization of how she looked hit me. Then I turned my head and looked across the waiting room at Emily – she was doing the same thing!

My daughter and this woman felt shame, like it was their fault that this terrible thing had happened to them. So here I was that evening sitting on the end of my bed staring at the wall feeling heartbroken.

My first intention was to drink, because it would be so easy to step back into my alcoholic ways. However, a voice popped into my head saying, "yes, but what would that solve?"

So I stood up and unpacked my boxes, which I had not yet unpacked from moving house 4 weeks earlier. At the bottom of the box was a book staring at me. This book then led me to a film, which then lead me to Jack Canfield.

I have had to drag myself up from one step to the next on my journey to success. I have had to completely change who I was to become who I am now. So when anyone tells you that success is easy, they are lying. It's the love I have for my children, overcoming 20 years of domestic violence, overcoming drug and drink addictions, and the memory of that women's tear stained face that keeps the fires burning deep down inside of me.

I urge you to take on this rule of five just like I did and just like I keep doing every single day of my life. Two years ago I could only dream of being an International Best Selling Author, and now I am one.

Two years ago I could only dream of having my voice heard, and now it is GLOBALLY!

Two years ago I could only dream of my daughter climbing out of her dark hole. Now she writes, speaks and supports other teenagers who have experienced dating abuse. She even came to me and asked me to interview her live on my Internet TV show so that she could show the world that you no longer have to hide and feel ashamed.

This rule of five has now placed a footprint on humanity and also on my children's lives too. They now realize that your dreams can be fulfilled because their mother is living proof. Working on you is not a selfish nature. It's creating foundations for those who look up to you and giving them hope.

I hope you to take the rule of five into your life and just complete 5 small goals a day. These goals won't take you much longer than a few minutes each day. The results are astounding. Take this book for example!

I now know that I had to walk a path of pain for 20 years to deliver this amazing book to you!

Would I do it again? Yes!

Lil Lezarre

I am 49 years old, and the past 11 years have been the best of my life. I have a full-time job with a great employer, a romantic relationship that keeps getting better, happy healthy kids and own my own business, a bra shop, which I started 3 years ago. I am active on the parent council at my daughter's school and with the ACC, which I currently chair.

www.lilsprofessionalbrafitting.ca

✉ **lil@lilspbf.ca**

f **facebook.com/pages/Lils-Professional-Bra-Fitting/215675105173124**

🐦 **twitter.com/LilsProFitN**

CHAPTER 2

BE YOURSELF – AMAZING THINGS CAN HAPPEN

By Lil Lezarre

At the age of 16 I ran away from home with my ex-husband to escape the brain washing religion of Jehovah's Witnesses and ran into 22 years of emotional abuse. I clearly remember the feeling of being trapped; nothing left of me, with three children, then aged 4, 6 and 8. I was only functioning day to day. I couldn't see a way out, but his behavior was escalating and he started spanking the kids.

Nov 18, 2002, was the day I packed up the kids and ran into the WIN house. I have no doubt we would not be alive today had I not left. I'm so thrilled to have this opportunity to share my story and let you know how great life can be even after serious long-term damage to your self-esteem and self-confidence.

Gone are the days of wishful dreaming. Anything I want I make a plan and make it happen; it's my choice. It's been a long journey and a lot of work, but it's all made me who I am today – happy, healthy and eager to help other women turn their lives around.

I've surrounded myself with positive supportive people, and this chapter is about these wonderful people who help make my life the best it's ever been (a statement I keep repeating every time I look back). I think my life couldn't get any better – then I look back and repeat "life is the best it's ever been."

Natalka Breckenridge: I worked for Natalka in the early 80's and I'll always remember the letter she wrote to me advising me to get out – that I deserved better. Natalka was also one of the ladies crucial in helping me leave my ex-husband. She lent me the money to buy my first car after leaving, and in 2013 provided me store space in her company's warehouse for my bra shop. I remember she called me a couple weeks after I left asking if I had any regrets; my answer was "I'm afraid I'm going to wake up." The only problem with Natalka is she won't take anything in return. I owe you so much Natalka. I've always been impressed with your business success and so lucky to have you as a friend. You're one of the nicest people I know.

Michael Lezarre: You are the most honest, open, respectful, positive, supportive, modest and compassionate person I know, and I'm so lucky to have you as a partner. Our relationship is very unique. We met in 2005 online at Lava Life, and our first conversation consisted of him passionately describing the ice at Maligne Canyon. At the time I was only looking for adult companionship and adventures in the mountains. With two children under 10 living with me, that's the only time I wanted a man in my life, otherwise I needed my freedom. We have countless stories of our adventures in the mountains and many sore stomachs from laughing so hard. I was able to move from low income housing when we bought a house together in 2009 and have the healthiest relationship imaginable (and still creating more memories and enjoying laughing sessions). Michael, you are the reason for my high self-confidence and self-esteem levels. You are always telling me how great you think I am, and I know it's coming from your heart. You always look at things from the other side and have given me a new perspective. You have made me comfortable with who I am, and you are always ready to help with anything I throw at you. I wouldn't have started Lil's Professional Bra Fitting without your support. I want to grow old loving you.

Alpine Club of Canada-Edmonton Section (ACC): Michael introduced me to the best club in the world, and being a member has done so much for my personal growth. It's a volunteer organization, so if you're willing to put work into something, you are free to run with it. I love this club and send a huge "thank you" for everything it has done for me. Having joined in 2006, I was pleased to be invited to join the Board, and am particularly honored to be club chair for the 2012-14 term.

Donna McColl: My best gal pal, rock and ice climbing buddy, skiing buddy and now my marketing guru. Donna, you always have the best way of saying what a great job I'm doing on everything (she describes me better than I can). You came up with the name "Chicks with Picks" and "We Women Rock" for our girls only rock and ice climbing weekends. You also came up with the catchy phrase "Get out of Boob Jail and go to the Bra Spa" (hence why she's my Marketing Guru). You are also the reason for my upped business confidence, and I'm so lucky to have you as a friend.

Paragi Shah: My other best gal pal. P is a very successful sales manager for a diagnostics company and hosted my first bra party, which launched my home party business. You always impress me with the effort you put into keeping in touch with everyone (including me), your professional success and your commitment to charitable service with One International.

My children: Stiel, Cole and Shae: I haven't told you everything that went on leading up to me running away with you, and I'll have that conversation when you want it; just know that I love you all very much and always will. The hardest time in my life is when I lost all three of you to your dad, despite my best efforts in the courts. Many tears were shed through years of heartache and that's the only time I've had to deal with depression, but having you back in my life wouldn't be as sweet as it is without that heartache.

Shae: You were the first to figure out your dad and move back with me. I think we have the best mother/daughter relationship possible. You always impress me with your maturity (yes, I said maturity). I love your spunk, honesty and your humor. You have so many talents, and I'm glad I can give you the opportunity to explore them.

Cole: You were the first to give me tears of joy when, after 5 years of estrangement, you accepted my invitation for supper in November 2012. It was a dream come true when we resumed the fun of going on our skiing/boarding trips together. You've developed your educational goals on your own and are on the right path with pursuing them. I'm so glad you've welcomed me back into your life, and it's the coolest thing that we share a passion for the mountains.

Stiel: It pained me to miss your childhood, and as I get to know you now, your maturity level at 18 years old is staggering. Your ability to see the positive in all of your hard knock life lessons is an attribute that will serve you well all your life. You shouldn't have learned those lessons from your father, but it's all part of who you are today. It's so sweet for me to see your interest in climbing, and really cool I can share my love of it and of you as I teach you the sport. You impress the hell out of me every time we talk on a trip.

Dorothy Briggs: This woman is all about networking and helping you grow your business. Dorothy, I am in awe of the passion and love you have for what you do. You have shown me the importance of presenting myself in a professional manner and giving back to the community. I have had to push my boundaries since the first time I met you at the luncheon when you wouldn't let me sit by the only person I knew. You invited me to the first meeting for the Breast Event Ever, and now I'm on the sponsorship list for the Edmonton Dream Centre. You are the reason for my professional growth.

Shane Dobson: My best bud. We used to work together, and he supported me through my divorce and losing my kids. We're still good friends, and yes, when you're in a healthy relationship, it's OK to have guy friends.

My lesson – "Do what's right for you." You will never feel that total contentment inside unless you have the freedom to follow your heart and your passion. I don't know how to explain it, but doors just open – you meet the right people and things happen. You want to be in the positive circle and the domino effect happens in a positive way.

If you're in an abusive relationship – get out. That's the only answer. A controlling, manipulative, jealous person will never truly support you (they have a way of making you feel supported but they're not. It's like a competition to them and they must win.). This goes for all relationships, including friendships. Friends are important in supporting you through the tough times, but just as important is sharing the good times and being excited for you and your accomplishments (and vice versa).

Do what's right for you. Follow your heart and your passion.

A good counselor is very important for your road to success; keep looking until you find one that connects with you. When every day is a struggle, we beat ourselves up too much and prevent our own growth. You have to be comfortable being open about everything before they can help you. One of my best counselors showed me how to be compassionate with myself (a huge step).

Being free affects us in so many ways. Be with people who share your values and support your ideas. When you're not, you normalize what you are not, and that slowly eats away your true self. It's great being able to say what I'm thinking without any worries that it will be misinterpreted; I don't have to cautiously say what happened today.

As I finish writing this chapter, I look back and once again, life is the best it's ever been!

Erica Gordon MA, CPC

Erica has four beautiful children and a gift to inspire women facing challenges. After healing from a devastating divorce, Erica made it her mission to empower women. She shares her personal journey of self-discovery to teach women to live fully by reconnecting with themselves and their dreams. Erica is a certified life coach with a Master's in psychology and executive coaching, CEO of Defining Success, LLC, and founder of Moms with D.R.E.A.M.S., a "mom's network."

www.definingsuccessllc.com (coming soon)

www.meetup.com/Moms-with-D-R-E-A-M-S

Ericaglam (Instagram)

- **gord930@aol.com**
- **definingsuccessllc@gmail.com**
- **facebook.com/EricaGordon42**
- **facebook.com/DefiningSuccessLlc**
- **Twitter.com/CoachEricaG**
- **linkedin.com/in/ericagordon1**

CHAPTER 3

A JOURNEY OF SELF-DISCOVERY

By Erica Gordon MA, CPC

It was a beautiful sunny morning in May and the day of our youngest son, Eric's, sixth birthday party. I should have been filled with excitement for the celebration that we had planned for our little man. Instead, I was an emotional wreck, lying in bed desperately thinking, "this has to be a bad joke – in any minute he's going to tell me that he's just kidding…" Not once in a million years did I think that this would happen to me.

I dedicated my life to this man and vowed to stay with him through sickness and in health. I took my wedding vows and marriage more seriously than many of the people I knew. When I realized that this wasn't a joke, I began to feel weak, sick, and out of sorts – almost like I was having an out of body experience. Completely devastated and in shock is the best way I can describe how I felt in that moment. The bomb that he dropped on me was too much for me to handle. I had always been strong and resourceful when faced with challenges, but I didn't know how I was going to get over this one.

HOW IT ALL BEGAN

I became a mother at the tender age of 17, so I knew how to be strong and resourceful. Although I had my son, Khalil, in my senior year of high school, I was determined to graduate on time and still go to college. I knew that I could accomplish those goals as long as I remained focused and didn't give up. After graduating high school, I started working full-time as a bank teller and attended Rutgers University part-time, taking classes at night. Although I had very little support, I found a way to make it work. Rutgers had an evening child care facility where I would drop my son off on Tuesday and Thursday evenings while I hurried off to class. Despite my circumstances, I was focused and navigating well, until I met the man who would change my life forever.

In July 1997 I unexpectedly met a man who instantly swept me off of my feet. I was tired of dating immature guys who couldn't accept my independence and responsibilities as a single mom. My soon-to-be husband was also tired of the dating game and convinced me that he was ready to settle down. Against my parents' and grandparents' wishes, we were married three months later by the justice of the peace.

Our family grew by leaps and bounds. I gave birth to our daughter, Niara, in November 1998, our first son together, Sharif Jr. in November 1999, and our last son, Eric, in May 2001. One month before Eric's first birthday, we became proud homeowners. We were young and happy – or so I thought. While I was busy taking care of our young children, managing our household, working, and taking online classes, my husband was busy creating a separate life of his own. His secret double life revolved around young, single friends with no ambition or any real direction for their lives. He spent the majority of his time away from our children and me. He would feed me lies like he had to work late, or he was "hanging with his boys and lost track of time." Well, as the saying goes, "what's done in the dark will eventually come to light."

LIVING IN FEAR AND LONELINESS

On that dreadful morning in May he casually told me that he had been cheating with a woman that I had known to be a friend, and that her daughter was possibly his. I literally felt like I was going to die. For the next year my life was a living hell as I struggled to maintain the façade of our perfect life while I was dying inside. The pain was unrelenting, and I could not get rid of thoughts of him being intimate with and loving another woman. Although I tried to make our marriage work, I could not forgive him and we eventually divorced.

The early days after my divorce were often unbearable. I would cry incessantly and couldn't eat. I stayed frustrated, overwhelmed, resentful, and had no patience for my children. I felt hopeless, sad, lonely, afraid, and blamed myself for my failed marriage. I knew that I had to pull myself out of that slump for the sake and wellbeing of my children. I didn't want them to feel like I didn't love them and that they were the reason why mommy and daddy were divorced.

THE REAWAKENING OF MY SOUL

It took four years for me to regain my balance, inner peace, and reconnect with myself. Along the way I realized that my situation was bigger than me and that I needed to ask for help. Although I knew that I was strong, I realized that I was going to need support if I wanted to save my life and take care of my children. If I had not made the decision to take back my life, I may not be here sharing this story right now. The method that I used to reawaken my soul and start living again is what I call my signature D.R.E.A.M.S. Plan. This is a six-step process for women who face challenging, life-changing circumstances or events that have caused them to feel off-center and out of touch with themselves. I know for a fact that these six steps saved my life, and they can help you save yours, too.

1. **D – Decide** that you are worthy of being happy, healthy, and complete. Decide that you will no longer allow fear, loneliness, guilt, self-loathing, or blame to have power over your life anymore. Once you make this decision, you have to resist defeating, limiting beliefs that speak about your past or current circumstances, and that try to predict your future. Declare that everything that has happened to you in the past has made you into the powerful woman that you are today.

2. **R – Reach** out for support and guidance and cultivate healthy relationships. Record your thoughts in a journal and remember that you are not alone. I sought the help of a few therapists to help me through different stages of my healing process. I strengthened my relationship with God and asked him to guide me and direct my steps. I started writing in a journal, which was therapeutic when I didn't want to talk to anyone. Lastly, I leaned on people in my circle who genuinely cared and wanted the best for me.

3. **E – Embrace** who you are and forgive yourself for any past mistakes. Make a list of your greatest qualities, things you do well with no effort, things that people compliment you on, things people ask you to do for them, etc. You will develop

an admiration for yourself once you rediscover and embrace how you shine your light on the world.

4. **A – Affirmations** – after you list all of your great qualities, create daily affirmations that speak of your greatness and exemplify how you are living your best life now. You can also make affirmations that encourage and inspire you. One of my favorite affirmations is the Bible scripture, "I can do all things through Christ who strengthens me."

5. **M – Make** yourself your number one priority. Self-care and self-love are so important. For years I put my children and husband before myself and never thought twice about it. I would rarely buy myself anything and would feel guilty if I did. Scheduling time for you is an essential part of your healing process. I want you to start loving and caring for yourself so you can love those around you. What can you do for yourself today?

6. **S – Start where you are** – begin taking these small steps today in the direction of becoming a whole, healthy woman, so you can stand on your story and not in it. Often times we wonder why hurtful things have happened to us. It may not be for you to know while you are going through it, but there is always a reason. In my case, I learned that I went through this painful experience so I could use my story to empower and support other women to live fully in their greatness.

Your journey to self-discovery will be exciting and may feel a little scary at times. By applying these six simple steps you can also reawaken your soul and discover your true essence. I didn't understand the value of taking care of myself until I was forced to make a decision about how I wanted to live the rest of my life. I had two choices – to wallow in my misery or get up and take control of my happiness. I chose to take a stand for my life. I discovered that I deserve to be happy and live the life I desire, and so do you. I leave you with my mantra that I hope you will apply to your life: "If I can do it, you can do it, too."

Andréa Dykstra

Andréa Dykstra refers to herself as a Storyteller rather than an Author/ Speaker, and she shares her stories to initiate healing transformation within others.

Kidnapped, raped before her third birthday, sexually abused, and mentally, physically and emotionally abused for nearly three decades; Andréa passionately believes that we can heal anything!

As an intuitive and Master Life Coach (AUNLP), Andréa uses her experiences to guide trauma survivors, and women and men facing challenges on their life's journey, to a place of forgiveness, trust, gratitude, joy, and love.

Andréa's passion, and her gift, is to inspire you, empower you, and support you to set yourself free!

www.andreadykstra.com

www.plus.google.com – Andréa Dykstra

✉ **info.andreadykstra@gmail.com**

f **facebook.com/groups/BoundlessGoddess**

⊕ **pinterest.com/andradykstra8**

○ **twitter.com/EnergizedLife**

▶ **youtube.com/user/alphadretti**

in **linkedin.com – Andréa Dykstra**

CHAPTER 4

I'M NOT AFRAID OF THE DARK...

By Andréa Dykstra

I awake in my darkened room.

What was that sound?

My eyes are drawn to a faint glimmer. There's someone in my room!

Oh my God, there's someone in my room!

Moonlight glints off of a knife. My breath stops. Fear is lodged in my throat. The hint of movement, the knife moves closer; my killer's body is still shadow upon shadow. I lay paralyzed with fear, inert, immobile.

I can only watch as the minutes tick by, and the knife moves ever closer.

I envision my ten-year old body torn open by the blade, never knowing…is it my brother? Is it my father? Maybe it is one of my mom's many boyfriends, or just a stranger. The only thing for certain is that it is a "he." Experience has taught me that men hurt, and they lie, and they take, and they punish.

I lay motionless.

Time ceases to exist except in the movements that shift him ever closer to me. I am returned to my primal state; all tactile and heightened senses. Adrenaline floods my body. I'm too young to understand the adrenal feedback loop – the hypothalamus triggering the pituitary gland to stimulate the adrenals into response.

I feel my veins turn to fire and ice, the result of cortisol racing through my body. My limbs are tingling and numb as the blood retreats from my extremities to protect my vital organs. My vision is heightened, my hearing acute; I am a lion ready to pounce!

I decide not to wait for death to come to me.

Without warning, I leap out of bed and reach past the knife as I lunge for the door!

Ecstasy fills me as I feel the doorknob, warm in the palm of my hand. I yank on it with the super-human strength that seems to flood my body.

In my haste, I forget to twist the knob.

I am thrown forward as I meet with resistance, and my head snaps back and then forward on my neck; jolting me. With a savage cry, more feline than human, I crank the handle to the right and throw open the door.

As I instinctively duck to move around the door, I run my hand up the familiar wall and scrape the light switch on while I continue my forward momentum. I run for the bathroom, and the safety of its locking door.

I don't look back.

I push into the bathroom and throw my small body against the door as I stab the locking handle in with a thrust!

Seeking more solace than the glow of the nightlight, I turn on the overhead light and back away from the door.

I wait.

Surely my mom will wake up; she must have heard my hasty exit and primal scream, or the slamming of the bathroom door.

Nothing.

My frantic little girl's mind fills with nightmarish thoughts. What if he's already killed her? What if I'm alone? How long before he breaks down the door?

I edge back toward the door, slowly, silently, listening.

I can't hear anything, nor can I see any shadows from the thin crack beneath the door. I back away and scan the room for a weapon, anything that can be used for protection.

I find nothing.

I am overcome by a sudden fear – that he has his eye pressed up beneath the door looking at my feet, and will figure out a way somehow to be able to reach through that impossibly thin crack and hurt me.

I climb into the bathtub, and I wait, every second stretching out into an impossibly long silence.

I don't dare go out. I don't dare exhale…

My pelvic floor muscles are so tight that the physiotherapist can barely insert one finger into my vagina. I draw my breath in sharply as she presses her finger inside. I contract, resisting the pressure, fighting the intrusion into my sacred space.

I try to alleviate some of the discomfort by joking with her that I have been holding my breath since I was two and a half years old (when I was kidnapped, but I don't tell her that part).

It's not very funny as I lay here on this cold table with her fingers inserted first inside my vagina and then my anus, trying to gently coerce my pelvic floor muscles into relaxing, into lessening their choking hold on my body and my life.

I have come to her to try and put an end to the excruciating nerve pain that has taken control of my life. Some days it hurts to even have clothing touch my body, the lightest whisper of a bed sheet sending me into spasms of pain.

I feel as if the top layer of my skin has been torn off and the exposed nerve endings are having acid poured over them, while I am being savagely torn apart by some wild animal's teeth.

In addition to the physiotherapy, I also end up having to learn how to breathe again.

My diaphragm has become stuck, frozen by fear, it is not moving in synergy with my pelvic floor muscles. Essentially, I am being pulled apart from inside.

The doctors and specialists are unable to find the cause. Nothing that they have given me can lessen the pain; I live in a constant state of a heightened nervous system, not able to relax. I have tried everything from mainstream medicine to ancient Eastern wisdom, and several alternative-healing modalities, with little relief.

My final surrender is to disassociate myself from my body, to try to exist outside of the pain, separate.

I manage this separateness for years. I even convince myself that this dulled existence is a very spiritual way of life. However, rather than detaching myself from the pain, I was actually denying it.

This meant that I had also separated myself from an awareness of myself as a physical body.

From the outside, my life looked incredible and full. The casual observer would not notice the strain that the constant tension of denying a part of myself, refusing to look at the fear, was causing.

I, myself, did not understand that I was undermining my very Soul by denying my physical body.

The strain finally revealed itself in the form of Adrenal Fatigue, which I became fond of referring to as "mostly dead." The nature of it is that it robs you of your life, while you still live.

The underlying cause of the Adrenal Fatigue was Complex Post Traumatic Stress Disorder (CPTSD), a little known form of trauma that affects kidnap victims, childhood sexual abuse victims, and concentration camp survivors or prisoners of war.

I was both a kidnap victim and a childhood sexual abuse victim.

I had been suffering from this traumatic disorder nearly my whole life. It took the manifestation of the Adrenal Fatigue in order for me to finally uncover the root cause of my suffering. This suffering had affected aspects of my physical, mental, and emotional bodies.

35

In order to fully heal, I made a decision to return to the pain.

I initiated a process that I refer to as "Touching the FEAR." It is an exercise designed to bring awareness into an area where we are afraid to go, whether that is a memory, an event, a physical injury, a relationship, chronic pain, or an entire childhood.

My favorite acronym for "Fear" is "False Evidence Appearing Real." This process is designed to reveal the illusion of fear, and in doing so dismantle the hold that it has on us.

TOUCHING THE FEAR

Create Safe Space

It is important to first establish a safe space; a place that is comfortable and where you will feel protected. If this means leaving your home, do so.

It can be helpful to enlist a trusted friend or family member to sit with you and hold sacred space for this process.

Identify the Fear

Write this down on a piece of paper, or in your journal.

If you are dealing with a childhood fear, be sure to write it in the language of the little girl or boy, rather than trying to capture the essence from an adult perspective. Take the time to go within and ask your inner child what she or he has to say about the fear.

You may wish to begin with a paragraph, and then pare this down to a single succinct sentence, or even one word.

Breathe

It is important to establish a complete breath (see resource link below).

Allow the Fear

Close your eyes and focus on the sentence or word that you have written. Now, allow your mind to reach directly toward that fear.

You may have written that you are afraid of dying alone. Instead of recoiling at the thought (our normal reaction), we don't want to look at that possibility. Go directly toward what it is that you feel when you think of that scenario.

Observe

It is important during this exercise that you simply look, rather than becoming emotionally involved with the scenario. Remember, you are in a safe, protected space.

Physical Sensations

Where do you feel this in your body? Is your throat constricted? Do you have butterflies in your stomach? Does your back hurt?

The physical body is full of wisdom, and it is always speaking to us. Take the time to listen to where this fear is manifesting in your body.

Move around, chant, hum, yawn, or massage, stroke, or tap any areas that you feel compelled to. This is a great release for our cellular body, and chakratic system.

Identify Truth

As you allow yourself to look directly at your fear, you are going to be able to dismantle everything that your mind has told you about this fear.

If the fear was "dying alone," you are going to realize that this is an illusion created by a mind that feels unloved, or unlovable.

Open to Love

No matter what the fear you are dealing with, it is coming from the opposite space of love.

The mind will try to tell us that it is too risky, too painful, too vulnerable, yet we must allow ourselves to open to the vibration of love in order to fully heal. Allow yourself to feel the longing for love that has been masquerading as fear.

We may need to go through this process more than once for a particular fear. What determines the effectiveness of the process is our ability to observe the fear without becoming lost in it, and our willingness to open ourselves up to love to allow healing to occur.

You may be surprised to find that you can clear a long-standing fear with one session of "Touching the FEAR."

Clearing the fear of my ten year-old self, that of being stabbed to death, proved a bit easier. When I finally emerged from the bathroom later that night and made my way back into my bedroom, I found my mom's travel alarm clock staring at me from the dresser.

Its arms were coated with a glow in the dark substance (anyone who has seen Life of Pi, would recognize its twin in the ship's cabin where the family was bunked).

In the dark, the gleam from the arms could easily be mistaken for the glint of a knife, edging closer with each minute that ticked by. Well, at least to a kidnapped and abused child they could.

Resource Link:

www.andreadykstra.com/the-foundation-of-breathing.html

Tondra TanJuan Teej Mercer

Impacting the lives of millions through her storytelling, TaJuan "TeeJ" Mercer, an award-winning TV editor, seemed to live the good life. With an impressive Hollywood resume, TeeJ woke up one morning, after years of denial, and finally accepted that she had become a statistic. SHE WAS A BATTERED WIFE. Now, coined as "That Resilience Girl," TeeJ teaches women how to stand ON their stories as Thrivers, rather than IN their stories as victims.

www.TuesdaysWithTeeJ.com

facebook.com/ThatResilienceGirl

twitter.com/TaJuanMercer

CHAPTER 5

I DON'T FIX CRAZY

By Tondra Tajuan Teej Mercer

As a successful TV Editor for the last 20 years, I have been crafting stories for some of the biggest networks on television. For about four of those years, I harbored a dark humiliating secret that not even those closest to me knew.

You see, while I was holding it down in Hollywood, I was being held down in my own home.

I was a battered wife.

But I've gotten ahead of myself. So let me back up a minute.

One of the most dreaded stages of television production is getting the network notes, in other words, the changes that the network wants to make on your show. This stage is really no fun and some of the notes leave me scratching my head with sheer befuddlement. Sometimes the changes seem so drastic I find myself thinking, "now that's just plain crAzy."

One day, several years ago, that simple thought was the catalyst for one of my greatest personal paradigm shifts. It was a typical day and the network notes had just come in while I was in my colleague's edit bay. His name is Kurt, and I affectionately call him my work husband. Kurt and I were reading our notes when I came across one that just perplexed me. It was contradictory and made absolutely no sense. I usually try to keep my unflattering opinions to myself, but apparently I was so appalled by this particular note that it slipped out of mouth, "that is crAzy, and I don't fix crAzy" ran through my mind. I didn't realize that I had actually said it out loud until Kurt's uproarious laughter interrupted my musings.

To be sure he'd heard right, through hysterical laughter he managed, "TeeJ, did you just say you don't fix crAzy?" Confused as to what had tickled his funny bone so deeply, I hesitantly replied, "yes," and he laughed even harder.

While I didn't get the hilarity in it, somehow it stuck. And "I don't fix crAzy" quickly became our workplace mantra, following me to subsequent shows. I still have assistants who text me reminding me, "TeeJ, I remember what you taught me. 'I Don't Fix crAzy.'"

However, "I don't fix crAzy" took on a whole other meaning when I woke up one morning and realized for almost four years, I had been sleeping next to crAzy!

I revealed earlier that I was a battered wife, but allow me to make an adjustment to that admission. I was a 6-Figure battered wife!

Why did I make that distinction?

Well in my naive head, domestic violence only happened to low income, uneducated women with low self-esteem. This could NOT possibly be happening to a Howard University-educated, high earning, overachieving, highly respected woman like myself. NOOOOOO! That could never happen to someone like me.

Boy was I clueless. Now, I describe it as "I had educated and successified (yup, made up a word) my way into denial." Plus, I was not a quitter. That was MY missing piece. It took me a minute to grasp that getting out of the marriage did NOT make me a quitter. It made me a survivor.

Where did your transformation journey begin, you may ask.

Well, it began with two epiphanies.

THE FIRST EPIPHANY

Around August of 2009, I had just gotten home from working 36 hours straight. Yes, I know. Those are doctor's hours. But sometimes creating a television show is like diagnosing a trauma, and then doing whatever it takes to "save" it.

Meanwhile, my ex-husband, who had not worked in a couple of years, was standing in the kitchen. Understand that this was before the economy tanked and jobs were still attainable. He just kept getting fired. I came in exhausted with my eyes focused on my bed. I threw my stuff down anywhere because all I wanted to do was sleep. And this unemployed man formed his little lips to yell, "OMG TeeJ, you are so lazy!"

What the what? Did he just call ME lazy?

I've got a job and have managed to keep it. I was completely dumbfounded and speechless. I didn't comment on how in the world he could call me lazy when I was the one going to work all day and not hanging out in the streets. In that moment, it was clear: THIS...MAN...IS...CRAZY. But, I said absolutely nothing.

With tears streaming down my face I turned on my heels, walked into the bedroom and got into my bed. Just before my head hit the pillow, I declared to myself, "That fool is crAzy, and I DON'T FIX CRAZY!"

THE SECOND EPIPHANY

Not long after the first one, around October of 2009, I'd worked a really long day and was looking forward to getting in my ultra comfy bed. I'd put on my favorite Victoria Secret flannel pajamas. They were sooooooo cute, multi-color bright plaid of my favorite colors.

15 minutes later.

My favorite pajamas were ripped and I found myself pinned against a wall grasping for air. My husband's hands were wrapped around my throat choking the life out of me. Unfortunately, this was not the first time. But this time was different. My husband's eyes had gone vacant. He'd completely checked out. His rage was so intense that he didn't even realize he was choking me.

Convinced I was going to die that night, I immediately saw my precious mother's face because I knew she had no idea what I had been living with. In fact, no one knew. It was my big secret.

I began to pray, "Lord, don't let me die like this. Don't let me die at the hands of this man. My mother and family wouldn't forgive themselves trying to figure out what signs they missed. I promise, if you get me out of this, I'm out of here."

And just like that, my ex-husband let me go.

After that umpteenth chance of God sparing my life, I finally woke up. I knew that if I didn't leave, this man would eventually kill me. In fact he once told me, "I will kill you, bury your body and go have a steak." So I knew I had to plan my escape.

It wasn't out of the ordinary for me to work long hours so I would stay at work until 2 or 3 in the morning and then when he got up in the morning, I'd pretend I was asleep until he left.

Before we met, my ex-husband was a major drug dealer in Los Angeles. Because of that history, if he felt like someone stole from him, there would be dire consequences.

Two weeks away from executing my exit strategy, my day of reckoning came on November 9, 2009. I was still keeping my head down and communication to a minimum. My ex-husband walked into the bedroom and handed me a stack of credit card debt that I did not know existed, to the tune of about $200,000. And it was in my name!

I was speechless and flabbergasted. I knew I had about $100,000 in my own personal savings and he had about $30,000, money I had helped him save. On the morning of the ninth, I called him on my way to work and told him I'd come up with a strategy to pay it down and I needed $20,000 of the money in his savings.

And do you not know what this man had the nerve to tell me? He told me NO!

I was shocked all over again and I lost it. We had the biggest argument and I really stepped completely out of myself. I cursed him plum out, and I typically don't curse. As soon as I got to work, I went right to the computer and transferred the money out of his savings directly to one of the credit cards.

When I did that, because of his drug-dealing history, I knew he would consider it theft because he was not rational. Although I was going to use money I helped him save, to pay off the debt HE accrued, he still would convince himself that I had stolen from him. My two-week exit strategy got moved up to THAT night. I knew I could not go home.

When I called him to tell him what I had done, he responded EXACTLY as I expected.

I knew I had a small window with the element of surprise because he was not going to be home until very late. I seized that opportunity to move out – out of my own home that I had purchased for my 25th birthday. My home that I still had to pay the mortgage on, as well as pay rent for an apartment, with $200,000 of debt looming over me. That was a dark period for me. I felt like I was drowning, BUT I knew I could not stop moving.

I worked 20-hour days, and stayed in an extended stay hotel while I looked for an apartment. I cut off ALL contact with my ex-husband. I ignored calls, texts, and emails. I refused to let myself feel anything but rather I had tunnel vision as I went into a "I must survive, get somewhere safe and situated" mindset.

I kept up this insane schedule for an entire month. And I did not cry one time. Not one time!

I did not have time to cry.

But on that first night alone when I moved into my apartment, I finally let the volcano erupt as exhaustion reality hit me like a mac truck. I'd held it together for weeks, but I could not fight back the tears any longer. And the floodgates opened. Everything I had dealt with for the past three years came out, and it was a freeing purge.

Two years later, in October 2011, the divorce was final, and I have not looked back.

During that two-year window, I found my missing piece. I entered what I now call Resilience Bootcamp. I realized that everybody has a Resilience Muscle®.

What is a resilience muscle? It's that muscle that we're born with. It's not something that you can see like a regular heart muscle or leg muscle, but it's there nonetheless. Think about watching a baby learn how to walk. When a baby falls, although it may sting, she may cry for second or two but she jumps right back up. That's a resilience muscle.

However, as we get older, life challenges knock us down. Each time we stay down longer because our resilience muscle has gotten weaker. But with the right exercise, you can strengthen it.

I started with my F.E.W.E.R.™ exercise.

Face

Everything

With

Expected

Resilience

You see, at my core I knew I was an overcomer. I began to embrace God's DEFINITION of me rather than my ex-husband's DESCRIPTION of me. Once I made that paradigm shift, my ex-husband's words began to lose power.

As God's children who are fearfully and wonderfully made in his image, we are entitled to resilience. It is guaranteed. Once I accepted that I could boldly Face Everything With Expected Resilience, my Resilience Muscle got stronger daily. Today, I am nowhere near the broken and wounded woman that I once was. I stand in my greatness and you can too.

How?

Start by identifying the C.R.A.Z.Y. and make small daily thought shifts.

C – Is he CRAFTY with making the irrational seem rational?

R – Does he REFUSE to accept responsibility for his actions and blame you for everything?

A – Does he ASSUME the role of sole decision-maker and disregard your opinions?

Z – Does he ZERO in on your flaws and mistakes, overlooking his own?

Y – Does he consistently YANK at the rug of your mental, physical, and spiritual stability?

The next time your abuser does something that fits into the crAzy formula, don't try to rationalize it. Just firmly declare it as crAzy. Then quietly say to yourself, "I don't fix crAzy." Hear me. Trying to rationalize crAzy will drive YOU crAzy, and crAzy belongs in your rearview mirror.

Let me show you tangible examples.

Crafty

HIM: TeeJ, you moved out and left me for dead.

MY THOUGHT: Well I left you $89,000, so that's crAzy and I Don't Fix CrAzy.

Refuse

HIM: TeeJ, if you knew how to talk to your husband, it wouldn't set me off.

MY THOUGHT: You are blaming me for your lack of self-control. That's crAzy and I Don't Fix crAzy.

Assume

HIM: TeeJ, you are going to buy me a $10,000 Breitling watch.

MY THOUGHT: You don't have a job! That's crAzy and I Don't Fix crAzy.

Zero

HIM: TeeJ, you have no common sense.

MY THOUGHT: Yet I'm in the one who can keep a job. That's crAzy and I Don't Fix CrAzy.

Yank

HIM: TeeJ, you walking around naked does nothing for me.

MY THOUGHT: Wow! That's a crAzy statement to say to your wife. I Don't Fix CrAzy

Your mental state won't make an 180-degree turn overnight, but keep making needle point moves, strengthen your Resilience Muscle, implement your F.E.W.E.R exercise, and you will begin to thrive as you stand ON your story as a survivor rather than IN your story as a victim.

Laurie Crookell

Laurie is an Internationally Published Author, writer, speaker, and empowerment consultant. She holds a BA in Economics, and works as a math and literacy specialist for children with learning differences. She has had her writing recognized in several writing competitions. Her essay, "Learning, Upside Down" won the 2010 Human Potential Nonfiction Writing Contest. Her picture books, "Aaron's Salmon" and "Frieda's Frogs" have been finalists in the Writers' Union of Canada Writing for Children Competition. Two more children's stories, "Saving the Seahorses" and "Jennifer's Got Pizzazz" were recently short-listed as finalists in the 2013 Surrey International Writers' Conference Writing Contest.

✉ **lauriecrookell@shaw.ca**

❶ **facebook.com/laurie.crookell**

❶ **facebook.com/LaurieCrookellAuthor**

CHAPTER 6

LOSING SUPERWOMAN – THE POWER OF SELF

By Laurie Crookell

My telephone rang. I shrugged off lazy-morning air, and answered.

"This is the hospital," a nurse explained. "Your husband has been in an accident. I'm sorry. We don't expect him to live."

I staggered, breath dangling on fate's doorstep. Something burst inside; wild emotions spinning into a black vortex, battering me, threatening to knock me over. No escape.

My four-year-old bounced in, her playful energy giggling. Somersaulting onto the bed, she knocked blankets and pillows askew. My hands trembled, betraying my outer calm.

The sirens. I heard them that morning. Autumn's red wove magic through my bedroom window. My youngest daughter curled beside me, Peter Rabbit opened to page four. I pulled up the duvet, covering us both, breathed in her little-girl smell. Her two-year-old hand nestled mine, smile dissipating morning's mist.

Amid daylight's wakening peace, the sirens weaved their haunting cry up the mountain. Their eerie wail slithered around my house, crept in through daybreak's window, jarring me, as if they knew me intimately.

I returned to reading Peter Rabbit. The sirens' taunt remained, mocking, until it was dispelled by my telephone.

One phone call. Life as I knew it, over.

The hospital's ever-gloomy mood accosted me at its entrance. I was waved to a tiny waiting room, a stiff, unwelcoming sofa greeting me. A doctor entered. He sat, as rigid as the vinyl chairs lining the room.

"Your husband has been hit by a car. He's sustained a severe traumatic brain injury," he said. "He has two skull fractures, and severe swelling of his brain."

Panic clawed, strangling me with its intensity. This wasn't real. They'd called the wrong person. My husband was at work. A knowing weariness spread across the doctor's face. "If he survives, and if he comes out of his coma, he'll remain a vegetable for the rest of his life."

Fear. I knew it, then. It didn't slither. It didn't threaten. It didn't intimidate. It leaped, gripping my throat, claiming me as its own, a hundred lightning bolts striking simultaneously.

I was led to my husband's room, a prisoner dragged to her cell. Pitiful stares from sterile uniforms greeted me. My eyes were drawn to his body. Machines surrounded him, probing with their invasive tubes. He did not move; his coma so deep, he lay corpse-like.

I sat by his side, waiting, wondering, trapped in limbo's nothingness. Minutes. Hours. Days. Nights. His coma gripped him, chained me to his side, my emotions shackled by a deathless fate.

I became intimate with the subject of brain injury. Problems with motor function, memory, language, judgment, social behavior, impulse and emotional control, attention span, organizational capacity, personality changes; the chain gathered weight, slithering around my soul.

For three weeks, his coma held him captive, before fully releasing him from its grasp. I arrived one day to discover two physiotherapists holding him on the edge of his bed. His body hung limp, like a marionette with broken strings. My heart twisted. I looked to his eyes, searching for familiarity, a recognizable spark. The eyes of a child stared back. My heart faltered. His physiotherapists questioned him, pointing to me, asking if he knew who I was.

51

He didn't. He didn't know his children. He didn't know himself. He was a 17-year-old, vice-president of marketing, captured by Russian spies, and imprisoned in some torture camp. That's what he said, with drunken-like slurring, confused language, and an unfamiliar voice I did not recognize. My heart wrenched, fractured by grief's raw sorrow.

Tragedy stole my life that day. I wanted to negotiate with it, cut a deal. Spare my husband's mind; in return, I'd meet tragedy's demands. But tragedy had already declared its demands. I longed to run, flee this scene of emotional horror. But this was only the beginning.

He was violent for a time; multiple straight jackets, tied to the bed, heavily drugged, security guard by his side 24/7. Sometimes it took six men to hold him down. Nurses, exasperated one day, asked if I could convince him to take his meds. Voice as soft as a rabbit's whisper, I tried.

Venomous anger seared his eyes. His fist lashed out. I recoiled, pills scattering across the floor, as I dodged anger's fury. In that moment, I understood. This was not the man I knew.

That night, I gazed upon my sleeping children's innocence, and wondered how we would survive this wrecking crane called "brain injury." It demolished everything. Nothing but debris left behind.

In time, his progress astounded. He relearned to walk, made significant strides with motor and emotional control, speech, social behaviors. But his personality and executive functioning were never the same. He didn't think the same. He didn't act the same. He didn't talk the same. He had different tastes, different emotional responses, different humor.

For six and a half years, I fought to bring him back, my trauma and personal grief a buried landmine that festered inside, until I could no longer feel. I dreaded getting out of bed. I dreaded coming home. I was dead inside.

Understanding arrived on owl's wings. The man I married died in that accident; claimed by tragedy's whim. Only his physical form remained. His mind replaced by a stranger. Never again did I see the eyes I once knew. My white-picket-fence life vanished with the fatal blow of a morning's car accident, our connection severed the moment he was hit by that car. No longer could I stay in the lie I was living.

I struggled for a year agonizing over my decision. Torn by guilt and compassion, I stayed, until I could do no more. In humble apology to myself and to him, I spoke my truth, and set myself free.

Yet this tragedy, born on a misty September's dawn, has been my greatest gift. Life happens, to lead us to our destiny and our truest joy. When we take ourselves out of the tragedy and see it as transformational, a process of growth moving us to a better life, tragedy loses its control over us. My personal motto, "When life throws you lemons, they're really chocolate chip cookies in disguise."

In my pre-accident life, I was seen as competent – the woman who wore a cape and dared to do it all, the woman others wanted me to be, as if this would somehow make me acceptable to the world. I sustained this long after the accident, driving myself to be who I was supposed to be, until hitting burnout levels. My ability to live to others' expectations vanished. Friends deserted me. My self-confidence plummeted.

Yet that's when my gift appeared. No glitzy packaging. No sparkly bows. It came within. I learned to love myself weak. I learned to love my real self, not the self others expected. I lost the Superwoman image, and found me. Life-changing experiences cause us to shed our false personas, so we can shine as our true selves. Only then do we find joy. Only then do we truly give.

FIVE E'S TO FINDING JOY AFTER TRAUMA

1. **ENTITLEMENT:** Believe you are entitled to happiness. This is not selfish. The happier you are, the happier those around you will be, and the more you will give in your own unique way.

2. **EXPECTATIONS:** Let go of expecting specific outcomes about the how or when. Focus on the goals and ideals that will bring you happiness. And you will be drawn to them.

3. **EMBRACE:** Embrace change. The more we fear it, the more challenging change becomes. Welcome it. Tap into your

sense of adventure. Enjoy the challenge. Discover how these changes will lead to greater happiness. Reflect back on your life. You've resolved every challenge you've faced. Believe in your ability to deal with whatever comes your way. There are no endings, only beginnings.

4. **EMOTIONS:** Your emotions are your closest friend. Listen to them. Learn to recognize your true emotions, not the ones you've been trained to have. When you feel happy, stop and ask yourself why. Discover which things in life bring you natural joy. Pay attention to your energy level. If you feel drained after an activity, it's not joyful. Gravitate to those things that make you feel alive. Forget what "should" make you happy. Focus on what motivates and energizes you.

5. **ENJOY:** Happiness is a choice. By channeling negative emotions, we can move out of our comfort zones and create our best life possible. We can choose happiness.

   When making those choices, use your mind to assess pros and cons, but also dig deep into your emotions. Try the coin flip trick, seriously. Heads is choice A; tails choice B. Now flip that coin. Pay attention to your reaction. Notice if you are happy with the outcome, or disappointed. Your reaction will tell you something, what you really want deep inside. Choose happiness.

   When torn between several options, consider what it is you most fear losing. This will provide a clue to your next step. Choose to thrive.

Finding "you" is the path to joy. Being "you" is the greatest gift you can give. Survival is an inherent human trait. Thriving is a choice. Through that choice, we create our future, a future that will become our present. This is only the beginning.

Aime Hutton

Aime Hutton is from Calgary, Alberta, Canada, and known to many as an inspirational speaker, facilitator, and best selling author. Speaking to all ages of women/girls to empower, she inspires them to be brave, bold, and celebrate their unique self, as well as educating and supporting the next generation about the warning signs of dating violence, and sharing her own journey as the Canadian Ambassador for the Freedom & Empowerment Teen Campaign.

www.wondergirlscamp.com

www.awakeninggodess.com

- aime@wondergirlscamp.com
- facebook.com/CalgaryWGCAlberta
- facebook.com/pages/Freedom-Empowerment-Teen-Campaign
- facebook.com/Awakening.Goddess.YYC
- twitter.com/AwakeningGoddes
- youtube.com/user/dracof24/
- pinterest.com/aimeh/
- linkedin.com/pub/aime-hutton/34/b4b/b76

CHAPTER 7

FUTURE HUSBAND?

By Aime Hutton

Many people look to me as an inspiration, the one that has it all together. Seen as an inspirational speaker who has audiences up and dancing in the halls, daring to be brave, bold, and step into their own spotlight. I'm also known as the Canadian Teen Ambassador for a global campaign about dating violence. Sharing with teens and young adults across the country the warning signs of dating abuse, and the different kinds of abuse. Empowering them that love shouldn't hurt! However, how did this all happen? Let me back up a second.

What is it about University that is so magical? Well, mostly it's a place to learn, to live away from home for many, to make new friends, and potentially meet your future husband. For many, living away from home is the scariest part for them. However, what if I share a story with you that the scariest part isn't living away from home? For me, it was actually being in a relationship where I thought I was going to be with my future husband.

"I did it! I got in! Mum! I've also been accepted to live on campus in residence!" Squealing into the phone to Mum at her work. My acceptance letter to attend Lakehead University, in Thunder Bay, Ontario, had just come in. She was very excited for me too.

The summer flew by, and by the time it was done, I had packed up my things and was in the car heading up to Thunder Bay, a sixteen-hour car ride away from my hometown in southwestern Ontario. The leaves on the trees were already starting to change to the crisp oranges, vibrant reds, and electrifying yellows. Saying goodbye to my parents was tough. Yet, I had no idea what was just around the corner.

University life started right away, meeting new friends, attending classes, and everyone was on their own in the first year. So the game began of finding that one who could be a match to have a relationship with, for the long term. That's what my friends who were a year ahead of me in school did. One found her future husband. They are still in a loving relationship together with a beautiful little girl.

A few months in, couples were starting to pop up, and finally I was in one too. He had sandy blond hair, amazing eyes, and a smile that was like mine, big and full of teeth. He was a referee in hockey, and also was a computer geek all at the same time, which I really liked. I was also athletic in swimming, and field hockey, yet I also could play the clarinet, and be a band geek. We seemed to complement each other nicely.

People speak of the honeymoon phase of being in a new relationship. We had one too; it lasted till sometime after Christmas. After the Christmas break, he wanted to know everywhere I was going. There was a time when I got a phone call early one Saturday morning from friends who lived off campus. It was a brisk morning, as I stood outside my dorm waiting for the car to show up. We had a great day, and I was excited to share with my friends what I had been up too. Upon my return, a fellow friend from the dorm scurried down the hallway yelling to my boyfriend "Aime's home, you can stop worrying now!"

"Where have you been? I was worried sick. I didn't see you go to bed the night before, and I didn't see you leave this morning. I thought you were dead in a ditch. I called the hospitals and even the police station worrying about you." Devon kissed me forcefully as he pulled me into his bedroom. Not knowing what to say, I said nothing. Devon was glaring at me, little beady eyes, and pursed lips, breathing quite forcefully.

Other times I saw his jealousy pop up. Sitting at my desk, going over my notes for exams with classical music playing softly in the background, Devon came into my room wanting to have a chat/study break. Looking at my pile of CDs, he put one at the bottom of the pile. In a low voice, he stared at the CD and not even looking at me said,

"I don't want to hear about any of the crap you did when you were in high school. I wasn't there with you."

Taking a quick breathe with wide eyes looking back at Devon, I stammered back to him, "Those were happy times for me."

Or his anger would bubble up. One time he got so angry that he whipped his keys off from around his neck and toward a friend of ours. I also saw his jealously and anger all at the same time too. It was a clear dark night when a group of us went out dancing to the pub on campus. I was enjoying the beat of the music, and the heat of the lights. Devon was upstairs watching intently as we all danced. Waving at him to join us, a thrust of his stubby arm and round finger pointing forcefully that I join him, I obeyed. Not wanting him to get angry in public. I followed him like a little lost puppy back to the dorms. The frosty air hit my lungs and I couldn't speak. Once inside the dorm he twisted me around backed me up against the wall and kissed me long and hard, while squeezing his hands around my neck. I froze, my body stiffened. I could smell his breath, and remembering to be still. "I love you. I don't want to be with anyone else but you!" he said is a raspy voice with his piercing blue eyes when he finished kissing me.

Friends started to worry; they thought I should leave him. I could not see what was going on. I loved him. I thought he was going to be my future husband. When the school year was getting closer to ending two friends of mine took me out to talk one night. "How do you feel now, Aime?" the taller of the two questioned me with her caring eyes and huge smile.

The other reached out for my hands that were shaking, squeezing them lightly and said soothingly, "You're okay, you're safe, we even have permission to leave out the back door if we need too."

It wasn't until I was home that spring that I was able to look at it. Mum gave me a questioning look when I was out for lunch with her after returning home. "I don't know Aime; I do not like that he wants to know where you are going all the time." I hadn't been able to say I love you to Devon in months. I wrote a letter to Devon expressing that I didn't want to be a couple anymore.

The years following years two, three, and four were like walking on eggshells. I kept going with one foot in front of the other, believing that I would get through it with help from friends. However, Devon had other plans. He would just appear in an area where I was. He stalked me, and was also friends with my friends too, so I didn't get to see them much.

My final year I lived with two of my friends on campus in a town house. A BBQ was planned, and Devon was invited. I ate my dinner in my room. My roommate knocked on my door, jutting her arm with the plate of food on it into my room. "You know, it's been three years, you should be over it by now." Choking back my tears I replied shaking my head no.

I did get over it though many years later by starting to talk about my experience to friends and in classes about personal power and relationships. Having friends who truly want to see the best in me, they believed in me.

That's my wish for you – that you overcome whatever it is you are dealing with. Here are three simple steps to take back your life so you can thrive!

Step one – just keep putting one foot in front of the other. No matter how small the step, just keep going. There are others around you that can be your guides in your own dark time.

Step two – believe in yourself. You can get through, you will get through. There is always light at the end of the tunnel. And find the light in YOU. Your light is inside.

Step three – let others help you. They can't read your mind if you don't ask, and if you do ask, then let them help YOU! People will want to help you.

Lori Kay Blake-Leighton

Lori Kay Blake-Leighton was born and raised in Northern California. After experiencing physical and mental abuse in her first marriage, she has made it her mission to help other women overcome their situations and stand on their own. Now residing in Washington State with her husband Shane, son Zack and granddaughter Dakota, she continues to support women's groups and organizations related to her cause. She has been happily married for almost 25 years.

Mailing address:
P.O. Box 368
Ferndale, WA 98248

lkblake.64@gmail.com

CHAPTER 8

TO THE EDGE AND BACK
By Lori Kay Blake-Leighton

It's amazing how teens think they know everything isn't it? "I can live on my own," "I know what I'm doing," "We are in love!"...blah, blah, blah. Sound familiar? Yep, that was me as well.

THE EDGE

My parents divorced when I was eight, and it devastated me. I loved my parents and little brother more than anything. My parents had done an excellent job keeping their problems from us. I think that's why it was hard for me to understand the divorce. I missed my dad very much. He was handsome, funny, and we were very close. I wouldn't learn until later his reputation with the ladies and his extreme 'boxing' abilities with the men.

In 1979 at age 15, I fell in love and by 16 I knew he was "the one." A few days before my 17th birthday, my mom asked if I still planned on quitting school to marry him. Because of my answer, I had to pack my bags and move out. She was devastated but of course I didn't know that at the time, I just thought she was furious. I had left my little brother behind and guilted my dad into signing for me in Reno. It was all about me and my happiness. I had no idea until later how many lives my decision had affected, including my own.

He was charming, cute and had a wonderful sense of humor, but he also had a bit of a bad boy image and I think that's what appealed to me the most (all qualities my father had). We had fun together and I felt like I could be myself. I had dated nice, shy, sensitive boys, and he was different. What could it hurt?

Over time, the relationship started to change. He became more possessive, controlling and then the invisible "grooming" started. "No more wearing make-up, no revealing clothing, no cutting your hair, no male friends," and eventually I was forced to even throw away my school yearbooks. After we married the behavior became much worse. "No drinking, smoking or cussing. I don't like you hanging out with your girlfriends, and I want YOU to personally tell them." They had been my friends since kindergarten, but I did what he demanded under duress and fear.

Alcohol has a way of changing a "nice guy" – or anyone for that matter – and he was no exception. It was mid-August 1981, just slightly over two months since we married. We were leaving the county fair, and he was drunk and getting belligerent with a carnie. I spoke up about his behavior, which included a curse word and found myself being grabbed by the throat and thrown against the hard metal hood of our car. The pain was horrible. I thought he'd broken my back and I was scared. I wanted to go home, to my REAL home, to my mom.

On the drive home I was threatened, yelled at and told if I wanted to go home to my mom, I would have to jump out because he wasn't stopping. Huddled up against the passenger door, with my fingers on the handle, I prayed for the strength to jump. It never came.

Afterward, I received that well-known phrase, "I'm sorry and it will never happen again," but the bruises from that night would be my initiation into this marriage. Sleeved shirts and foundation make-up were to become my closest friends off and on for the next six years. Depression and suicidal thoughts were a close second.

Through the craziness of being physically/mentally abused and emotionally stifled, I've learned some things. Not while the abuse was happening of course but when my brain had matured. Science says the human brain doesn't reach adulthood until between the ages of 21 and 25, but if you have been groomed or conditioned to think or feel a certain way, that maturity may come later, if at all. This is why many women stay in these situations far longer than most people would. They are taught through verbal abuse and physical violence that they could never survive on their own, that no other man would ever want them or the worst, 'If I can't have you, no one can.'

Being in an abusive relationship made me an instant therapist for others in similar situations. Of course, they didn't know I was walking in their shoes. No, that would make me a hypocrite. I could talk the talk, but I couldn't walk the walk. My own parents didn't even know until after my divorce.

Because I was conditioned to believe I no longer needed to wear make-up, cute clothes or cut my hair, I didn't realize until later that it was a way of keeping me down. Making me look dowdy would keep unwanted attention off the wife. I was constantly questioned on why I took so long at the grocery store or the gas station. He would check the mileage in the car and ask where the miles came from. These were all scare tactics and they worked on my weakened mind.

Part way through the marriage, I mustered up enough courage to bit by bit, add a little mascara or trim my hair. Over time I slowly LOOKED myself again but inside I hadn't changed. I still received the occasional physical altercation from time to time, but by then he had already started to see that I was not turning back. I believe that is when the doors of change started to open for me.

Fast forward to 1988. It was a beautiful sunny day in Washington State. I was standing in the open front door of the apartment we once shared. He was pulling out of the parking lot towing a small U-haul trailer behind his car. I waved good-bye and he waved back. I watched him drive down the street until he disappeared. That's last time I saw him.

Once inside, I closed the door and leaned up against it, a place where my head was once bashed up against, and I realized something: 'Today is the beginning of my NEW life!' A huge smile swept across my face. I was so ready for this chapter I could hardly contain myself. And so it began...

AND BACK

My life wasn't great after he left, but it was a huge step to improving it. I had to take on two extra jobs, go through bankruptcy, lose my car, and other issues, but it was worth it. My biggest problem was now my emotions. I hated him. I hated everything he had ever done to me, my family, my friends, even my pets. The hate was so strong it consumed me. I received counseling and medication, but it didn't go away.

It took years for me to come to this conclusion that every single thing we do, we see, we say, we touch, affects us somehow. It changes our lives, the people around us and the world in which we live.

After listening to others speak of Gandhi, Deepak Chopra, Maya Angelou and many others, I decided a mental and soulful change was worth a try. Changing the way I looked at something sounded too easy to be true, but over time I realized it worked. Getting others to do the same, well that is a totally different book!

I realized that had I not married the man I did, I wouldn't have moved to Washington State and met my soul mate. Had I not been physically abused, I may not be involved with other domestic abuse groups to help others. Had I not been mentally abused, I may not have fully understood the importance and fragility of a child's mind, which then led me to become a more sensitive and in tune mother. Not to say domestic violence is in any way acceptable.

Every rock wall I hit, I eventually broke down; and with the rubble, I made stepping stones. These stones have led me to where I am today, and now I know with every single thing I do, see, say and touch that I am adding to the path. I know I will still trip from time to time, but that will only make the walk that much more interesting.

I have long since forgiven him and have prayed that he has found peace within himself. Everyone has a story for being the way they are. I never knew his, but he has helped me become the woman I am today. Not all women will be able to relate to my story, but if a woman can dissect it and find something they can work with, then so be it.

You can go to the EDGE, close your eyes, teeter on your toes, wondering whether to give up and fall off, or you can take a deep breath, open your eyes, turn around and run like the wind BACK to your future. The choice is yours and it's all in the way YOU see it.

Kim Boudreau Smith

Kim is an International Business Consultant & Strategist, Speaker and International Best-Selling Author. Kim's company, Kim Boudreau Smith, Inc., is dedicated to support women entrepreneurs to step into living their dream life! To step stronger into their Bold selves, become Top Producers in their life and achieve the wanted results-Success! Kim teaches women how to sell like a woman, with love and integrity! Helping over 1,000 people successfully achieve healthier lifestyles with her first business, she is taking this extensive business knowledge and paying it forward; helping women entrepreneurs defy obstacles, stop settling for less, step into their boldness and enjoy success. Kim is a passionate believer in collaboration, providing opportunities for other women and has a desire to motivate and support others to achieve their best through taking a call to action and achieving extraordinary results.

Kim can be reached at:

www.kimbsmith.com

www.boldradiostation.com

✉ **kim@kimboudreausmith.com**

f **facebook.com/kboudreausmith**

f **facebook.com/KimBoudreauSmith?ref=hl**

🐦 **twitter.com/KimBSmithInc**

in **linkedin.com/in/kimboudreausmith/**

CHAPTER 9

FALLING ASLEEP AT THE WHEEL, HOW IT LITERALLY WOKE ME UP!

By Kim Boudreau Smith

In August 2008 on a gorgeous sunny day at twelve noon, I fell asleep at a major intersection one mile from my home, not once but twice. However, NO ONE WAS INJURED!

So let me paint this scenario for you: the intersection consists of an eight lane major road in Detroit called Woodward Avenue. This runs from Detroit out to Pontiac, a suburb of Detroit, and it is 21.48 miles long. Four lanes north and four lanes south. Got the image? I was at an intersection and my foot was on the brake waiting for the red light to turn green when my head fell forward which woke me up, but then I did it again within seconds. I proceeded to get a hold of myself, made it home, got out of my cute red car and looked at it like it was a tainted poison apple and ran into my home!

I stood in the middle of my family room and said: "What in the hell is going on?" Well, don't let me fool you, I knew. I was just in denial! I was a year and half away from my 50th birthday and really looking forward to this, but I was not going to make it in this FRAME OF MIND! Yes, frame of mind!

So here is where it began:

I was a corporate America rock star climbing ladders, breaking sales numbers, getting promotions, traveling and what a life I had – or so I thought. I had it taken away from me in seconds, completely blind-sided. My self-worth was based upon my title, how much I was making and what my life looked like! I did this based on all lies – yes, lies – and I was successful at it. However, I did not know at the time what was happening to me and to my health.

I was diagnosed with anxiety and exercise disordered (there is a label for everything) nine years ago, and now I know the *whys* of my past! I was living in the societal projection and not in my passion. I was exercising 3-4 hours a day on top of working 8-10 hour days in my career. I thought exercising that much was providing me energy, but what I really was doing was feeding my anxiety and my false life. This took me down!

Twenty plus years ago I began my fitness business; it somewhat fell into my lap, but there are NO ACCIDENTS or COINCIDENCES! I always taught aerobic classes as a part-time hobby while building my corporate career, so it made sense to begin a fitness business. At this point, I really knew I wanted out of corporate. I had been beaten up badly with businesses going out of business, not paying their debts, being terminated for no reason, and so much more. This is the universe at work doing her job and sending her messages; I just did not hear or know it at the time. I was still following the socially acceptable view of what I should be doing with my life.

After 2 years of working my "day job" and my fitness business at night, I made the leap and left corporate. Now, at this point in my life I was just married for the first time and I was the breadwinner, so we really had to be mindful about our financial situation. My husband was an accountant, so he took over the responsibility of managing the finances and setting up my corporation. If it wasn't for him, I am not sure I would have started my first business; he taught me a lot. At this juncture in my career, it was imperative to get out of my "day job," because I was crying every day at having to go to work. I learned quickly that I was hired because no women were in a managerial role with this company, so the women didn't care for me and the men in management left me out of all the meetings. Talk about being so isolated and feeling stuck between a rock and a hard place! I HATED IT!

So I launched a very lucrative and successful fitness business, but something was still missing…

A few years into our marriage I knew that it wasn't not going to work out, BUT I kept going to make it work because I was afraid. How would I go on? What would everyone think about me? Questions like these made me stay. I stayed through an injury that caused a 3-month stint of living in vertigo and lost hearing in my right ear. At this time my fitness business declined, but when I was feeling better I built it back up. I had to, because when I wasn't working, my husband stopped making deposits into our joint account, so I had no money to make a car payment, feed my dogs, buy groceries, and pay the phone bill. I had to ask for him to make my car payment, stop at the store to buy groceries and dog food. I remember one night when I was waiting for him to come home from work (I was still in vertigo and couldn't drive) he had stopped to eat on his way home and chose not to bring anything for me or my three Labs. He literally was starving us and controlling the money. Needless to say, our marriage ended about a year after that.

The point of all of this is that I still did not slow down to listen to my heart; I jumped back into survival mode instead of passionate/thrive mode. I let my anxiety continue to control my thoughts and my life. I went back to living in the "what I should be doing!" state.

So how did I discover I have anxiety and exercise disorder? Well, this amazing woman was placed into my life, and we took a journey together. Eve helped change my life. I remember one day when I was in her office she looked at me and said, "You have exercise disorder." I started laughing at her and said, "What the hell am I paying you for? I don't have that, give my money back!"

I was in denial and that denial made me really, really sick. I worked out so much I brought myself to chronic fatigue, and could not even climb stairs without feeling like I was having a heart attack; and I was in the best physical shape in my life at this time! Spiritually I was depleted, and let me tell you I thought I had it all under CONRTOL. Ha!

Coming back around to that day at the red light, it was me that spoke myself into a slumber. I had lost my lust and passion for living, mentally, spiritually and physically. I would wake up in the morning and think, "What my day is like? And when can I crawl back into bed?"

So here is what I did that day five years ago in August: I made phone calls to my village of support. I started increasing my practice of yoga. I investigated in furthering my education, which led me to a coaching certification. I stepped into a nine-month journey with a very special woman, Ellen. I became a co-facilitator to support other women choosing to do this for themselves as well. I got involved with Reaching Higher, a leadership course for high school kids and became a facilitator.

BUT MOST IMPORTANTLY...

I came clean with myself and stopped living lies. I built my career on lies, and my adult life was all a bunch of lies, which fed the anxiety and pushed the workouts! So I started to clean up my stuff, and I stopped living according to others' expectations of me. I stopped the lies and came clean, and I never looked back since that day at the red light!

I now live medication free. I balance my exercising with my life, and I have an amazing business, where burnout doesn't exist. My self-confidence is strengthened daily, and I put myself out there and take risks of being judged and ridiculed by others. When this happens as well as when people ask me: "are you crazy?" I know I am being ME! I am on course of my purpose, my soulful passionate purpose!

Ladies, there is no other way, and IT REALLY ROCKS Being Bold and Being YOU!

Gail Stroeher

Gail Stroeher was born in Nova Scotia and has two loving sons. She studied RMT, Hypnotherapy, travel and tourism, and had a successful RMT/ Hypnotherapy business for many years. In addition, she served as a summer nature guide showing whales out in the Bay of Fundy. Her desire is helping women and men through motivational speaking.

Please contact me by email:

 gailmaria@yahoo.com

Subject: love and forgiveness

Books and web sites that helped me heal are:

www.thejourney.com

www.hayhouse.com

www.davepelzer.com

CHAPTER 10

RUNNING BLIND NO MORE

By Gail Stroeher

I was born in Nova Scotia and raised by my Nanny along with my brother and sister. We were poor. Nanny used to make most of my clothes out of sacks. I was teased and made fun of in school daily and never felt good enough in school or at home. Even though I was teased and bullied, going to school was better than being at home. Nanny used to say, "What goes on in the home stays in the home or they will come and take you away." I wasn't sure who "they" were. This set me up to never talk. This became my belief system.

Mother used to come home off and on, and I was always glad to see her. She was my mother, and no matter what she did I always loved her. My mother suffered from schizophrenia and I constantly saw her making very poor life choices because of her illness.

One afternoon she sent me walking to the store a few miles away in the pouring rain to get her a pack of cigarettes. I was around eight then. I ran as fast as my little legs would go through trees, pasture, and onto the highway. I kept wiping my eyes and my face as the rain was pounding down. As I arrived at the store I had forgotten what brand cigarettes she wanted. I thought I picked the right one.

I was so happy to get home and I just knew mother would be glad to have her cigarettes. There I stood soaking wet with a big smile on my face passing her the cigarettes. Before I saw her hand coming she hit me across the face, and I fell down on the floor. "You know what cigarettes I asked you to get, so take those back to the God damned store and hurry your ass back."

It was still pouring rain and now my tears were added to it. I ran so fast thinking, "how could I have been so stupid? Now mummy is mad at me." Finally I got to the store after repeating her brand over and over while running. The storeowner offered me a ride. I was really glad.

When mother was home she would come into my bedroom at night with a flashlight and look in my underwear. I often wondered what she was looking for. I was just a little girl around five. She would sometimes ask, "has anyone ever touched you there?"

"No, Mommy" I would say.

I felt confused and not sure of what to say to her. Then, one night I had a nose bleed and wiped my nose on the back of my hand then wiped my hand across my underwear and went to sleep Mother came with the flashlight to check me and saw the blood. She hauled me out of bed and yelled to get downstairs. Then she yelled to her boyfriend to come to the living room. The fear I felt was and is sickening to this day. I was traumatized by my mother most of my life.

Another time mother came home with another boyfriend. I was older then. She would check for footprints in the hallway that lead to my bedroom. She would say, "I know what's going on here." I was still too young to understand. Around Christmas she hit me across the head, and my head hit the side of the water pump in the kitchen. She said, "I want you out of the house!" I didn't know what she was mad about. I wrote a note and put it on the kitchen table. I was going to drown myself in the Bay. I thought mother would find the note and say, "oh well, she is gone now."

I packed some clothes in a paper bag, and took my cat crying so hard and so afraid. It was getting dark and snow was falling. Kitty and me went to the old barn loft in the yard and would stay until morning.

Then I would just hitchhike like my mother did. I didn't know where to.

Meanwhile, a nice uncle had come to the house and had seen the note. He took it to the police. I woke up to the sounds of people calling my name and flashing lights. I saw all this through the cracks of the barn. I was afraid and scared. I piled hay on myself and hid. People would open the barn door and call my name, but I was too afraid to answer. My brother found me at daylight. Mother was with him.

"Oh dear, why would you scare us all like that?" she said. As afraid and hurt as I was, I liked how it felt when she hugged and kissed me. She told me not to tell the police what she had done as she washed the blood off my head. When the policeman came, he said, "your mother tells me you do this kind of thing all the time. We have a place for kids that do bad things." I could see mother watching from the back room, so I held my head down and said, "yes sir."

Uncle would come home from sea occasionally. I was so afraid of him. He would come home at Christmas and throw out all the tree ornaments. I remember watching the tinsel shine on the snow. When he was drunk he would throw me out of the house. Nanny would throw blankets out the window, and I would spend the night outside. When he would come home in the middle of the night hungry, I would get out of bed to make him something to eat, and then he would throw it to the dog.

I was painting Nanny's hallway green for her one time when my uncle came home drunk. He came in the hallway and said, "What the fuck is someone like you doing painting this house?" He took the can of green paint and poured it over my head. I ran out of the house down the country lane. I could not see or hear. I ran in the trees hitting one after another.

When I was caught, it was by a neighbor and his wife. They embraced me and took me to their house. They washed my hair out with turpentine. They said I didn't have to go back. I was old enough. I was surprised that they were aware of the abuse.

I moved to Alberta, married and had a family with two loving sons. When I left this marriage, frightened and having endured constant putdowns, I was very afraid and in pain. I was in trauma mode, running blind. Out of everything that I have ever been through, this was the hardest. I was there for 24 years.

I enrolled in a program for women in transition while staying with a cousin in British Columbia. I learned life skills, and with counseling I found my voice. At the end of this program my counselor said, "I am going to ask you to stand. I have never asked anyone else to do this." She hugged me and said "of all the women that came into this program, and there are many, you are at the very top." After all you have come through, you still love.

At Vancouver airport, in the crowd a bright light went from me to another lady. She came back and sat beside me. She asked, "Did you see what I just saw?"

"The light. Yes." I said.

"You are not going to believe this, but I'm here at a conference. I'm an editor," she said, "And you need to tell your story. You need to help other women going through trauma."

If you feel not good enough, shameful, alone or fragmented, do this meditation. Go to a quiet place in your home. Take three deep breaths. Close your eyes. See and feel yourself walking in a cold heavy bog. Feeling sad. Look up across at the bank, and there is someone looking at you. She is bright, kind and smiling at you. You wish you could be her. So happy. Look, she is reaching for you. Take her hand.

She helps you out of the bog. You look in her eyes and feel loved. She is you, the part of you that felt lost. She was always there, strong, confident. You take her back now, be with her. Take back your power feeling happy now and wide awake.

Never be afraid to talk to someone you trust or read books that motivate and inspire you. Your power is in your voice. Use it. Ask yourself what ever happened to that person to make him/ her act so mean? This will help you to forgive.

Love yourself. You are beautiful. God is love and so are you.

Maxine Browne

Maxine Browne is the author of *Years of Tears*. She has dedicated her life to increasing understanding of domestic violence and how to enjoy healthier relationships. In her workshops she tells stories of abuse and recovery that will inspire you to press past your present circumstances to create the life you want for your family.

Contact Maxine at

✉ **maxinebrowne@dv-recovery.com**

⬛ **urlm.in/rqft**

🐦 **twitter.com/maxinebrowne**

▶ **urlm.in/rqry**

CHAPTER 11

WHIRLWIND ROMANCE: RED FLAG YOU HAVE MET AN ABUSER

By Maxine Browne

One failed marriage and two kids later, I met a man who I thought was the answer to my prayers. He turned out to be my worst nightmare.

After my divorce, I had not dated for about five years. I had been busy raising my children and trying to keep our lives afloat. It was hard raising the kids on my own. I held down two jobs, and trying to do it alone was overwhelming.

John worked for my company's distributor in Mexico City, and I lived in the United States. When he suggested we correspond through letters, I thought it was a great idea. I would have a friend in Mexico. Cool!

We wrote letters for several months. It was nice hearing about where he lived. He sent me a few postcards. Fascinating!

One day, I told him that I finally felt as though I was ready to go out to dinner with someone. I was surprised when a Federal Express envelope arrived the next day containing an 18-page marriage proposal. Wowza!

The letter was full of biblical terminology and scriptural references. He said that I was his missing rib and that since he lived his life before God, he would always treat me with the utmost honor and respect.

It was so flattering. I felt like a fairy princess. In addition, I was a devout Christian. Everything in my life centered around my faith. I danced in a worship group. I played in the church band and sang in the choir. Now, this man was speaking the language of my faith, the very foundation of my life, and proposing marriage. It was an answer to my prayers! So, I agreed to marry him.

Let me say, that anyone who proposes marriage after a couple of dates has no idea how serious a commitment marriage is. That's like saying you can marry someone you know casually. Almost as if anyone will do (Hummm, Red Flag!).

We were engaged for nine months. It was a long-distance romance, and romance it was! We talked on the phone on Friday nights until the prepaid phone card ran out of minutes. At first it was for 10 minutes. Later, the calls lasted for hours.

We had a schedule of letters. We sent out a package via Express Mail on Wednesdays. This package contained a letter, photos and postcards. Later on, we even recorded cassette tapes for each other sending an audio letter. We recorded love songs and sent them to each other in the packages. Then, on Tuesdays we also faxed a letter to each other's job.

So, there were calls, letters, pictures, postcards – I thought I was getting to know John pretty well. However, it never occurred to me that he was hiding things, lying, or creating an image of himself that was not true.

Just for starters, six months into our engagement, and only two months before he came to the United States to marry me, he admitted that he was still married. I should have broken up with him right then and there. How can you ask someone to marry you, if you are still married to someone else? That meant he lied to me, was hiding things from me, was making a commitment he was in no position to make, and that he was willing to lie to get what he wanted. (Red Flag!) He said he had been fighting the divorce for six years and that it should go through any day (And this, too, was a lie.).

When I told a girlfriend about the situation, she told me he should straighten out his affairs before coming. That sounded like good advice, so I said as much to John. He had a complete meltdown. He cried so hard he could not speak. He hinted that he would commit suicide (Red Flag!) if he had to wait, saying that the loneliness was too much for him (Red Flag!). His temper tantrum was a huge red flag that I did not recognize at the time. I was in love with this man. Instead of using my head, my heart melted in compassion. I told him to come anyway.

Two months later he told me his divorce was final (another lie). He sold his car and caught a flight to my city. When I saw him with suitcase, boxes and his guitar, I remember thinking, "Maxine, I sure hope you know what you are doing." He left everything and moved. You had better make this work! We were married 13 days after the plane landed (Red Flag!).

There is so much I didn't see at the time that is crystal clear to me now that I have removed my rose colored glasses. For one thing, he was too good to be true. What do people say about that? If something seems too good to be true, it usually is. Well, this was the case with John.

John showered me with attention. He listened intently to everything I said. I thought that was because he was enraptured with me. Nah! He was gathering information. Every word I spoke about people, places and things was then twisted and used against me as ammunition. An innocent story I shared about someone in my life that I cared about became the reason why this person was a bad influence on me.

And, speaking of attention, what I thought was romantic about the schedule of letters and phone calls was actually a sign that he was controlling me by monopolizing my time. He knew where I was if I answered the phone and talked to him. He controlled my time and who I was with all the way from Mexico in the guise of romance. I was on the phone with him, or putting together the next package or recording tapes. It was subtle control. (Red Flag!)

He exhibited an urgency to marry. I was not pregnant. Why did we have to hurry to get married? Today, I believe that he held some type of belief that marriage is equivalent to possession. He had a need to possess me or claim me. It had nothing to do with what I wanted, which was to share my life with my spouse. His idea of marriage was to claim his property or to delineate territory or stake a claim of some sort. His actions after the marriage bore out this theory.

John promised that we would be a happy family. He said he would help me raise my two children. He painted such a blissful picture. But when he arrived, he was mean, dictatorial and controlling. My children quickly grew to hate him. If we had all been in the same geographical area, I would have learned that his own children did not have a great relationship with their father. So, what does that tell you? (Red Flag!)

John promised that he was going to take care of us. He was going to alleviate the pressure I was under caused by working two jobs. He was going to help. However, when he arrived, he refused to look for work. He insisted on creating his own business in sales. He purchased cars at auctions and sold them. He tried his hand at multi-level marketing. He then started his own business as an interpreter, which finally bore fruit. In the meantime, I worked in his businesses and paid for everything. I signed over my paychecks, and he controlled all of the finances. (Red Flag!)

QUESTIONS TO ASK YOURSELF:

1. Did you experience a whirlwind romance? What did that look like for you? And how did your love sweep you off your feet?

2. Did you ever feel pressured into a committed relationship right away? What amount of time is reasonable in which to declare you are going to have an exclusive relationship?

3. Are you avoiding or making excuses for things that you have seen in your partner that you did not like? Write down the things you have noticed that you do not like.

4. Are you willing to have a relationship with someone who lacks integrity? Does that work for you? Pay close attention to how you feel. It will answer the question for you. Write down what you feel.

Malaika Cohen

Malaika Cohen is a Motivational Speaker and International Best-Selling Author who is intensely dedicated to help people overcome abusive relationships. She has a passion for helping people tap into their own creative potential for life-changing results. Author of her powerful autobiography *Shackles: Overcoming Domestic Abuse – A Modern Day Taboo,* Shackles charts her personal struggle to walk free after 34 years of violence, to raise awareness of all aspects of domestic abuse and prove there is a way out.

www.malaikacohen.wix.com/malaikacohen

themalaikacohen.tumblr.com

📧 malaikacohen@gmail.com

📘 facebook.com/malaika.cohen

🐦 twitter.com/malaikacohen

📌 pinterest.com/malaikacohen

▶️ youtube.com/user/TheMalaikacohen

CHAPTER 12

IT'S POSSIBLE

By Malaika Cohen

Although the world is full of suffering, it is full also of the overcoming of it.

Helen Keller

Happiness is a choice. I say this with such emphasis, and such conviction, I have already walked a mile in your shoes, because for a long time I believed happiness was not meant to be for me; it was just for some of us, and not for all of us. Tragic events and circumstances happen to us, and sometimes we have no control; yet, it's not the events and circumstances that stop us from being happy, it's the state of our mind that stops us – our own beliefs and perceptions, how we feel and think over these situations, circumstances, and relationships that stop us from being happy. I invite you to join me on this self-discovery journey as you read through the pages and hopefully feel motivated and inspired to be become a successful person.

Shackles: Overcoming Domestic Abuse – A Modern Day Taboo is my powerful autobiography charting my battle to walk free from 34 years of domestic violence. *Shackles* is for anyone seeking to understand the devastating and de-humanizing consequences of domestic abuse. It's an incredibly detailed, personal and revealing testament of the daily, and weekly toll of systematic domestic abuse both physical and psychological. I share the intimate details of my life to prove there is life after abuse. And it can be a life of SAFETY, HOPE and HAPPINESS. Who we are is but a stepping stone to what we can become. With each new day, I have come to appreciate my freedom.

I would like to highlight the subjects of aftermath, overcoming, forgiveness, and finally, the steps to becoming a well-established and successful person. How did I make it safe and find inner peace? This was a long journey and it will be one for you too; it doesn't happen overnight. I am not going to tell you it's going to be easy, I am telling you it's going to be worth it.

First, I must stress the following: if you are still in an abusive relationship or at an unhappy stage in your life right now, the decision to leave and change is not an easy one to make; there will never be such a thing as a right time. Not making a decision is a decision, and it is vital to make the choice to leave – especially if there are children involved. We have a duty to protect our children.

I have always eagerly waited for this phase of my life to begin. Many times I have envisioned what it would be like to leave, to start a new chapter, to end all the madness, the guilt, fear, shame, and hopelessness and leave it all behind. When I finally did, I was overwhelmed by emotions and feelings of fear, which is referred to as "the unseen aftermath." You can be who you want to be right now, no matter what your situation looks like. Being unable to make decisions can cause you serious stress in your life; it can drain you of all your energy and willpower. However, you can do certain exercises that help you through the decision making process.

Life is about how we overcome and thrive through our trials. We must be tested in order to send the message to the universe that we are prepared for the blessings that await us. Happiness takes preparation and courage. I know you are hurting and you have been deeply disappointed, but it is our responsibility to make the choice that shapes the life we have.

It's called the healing process; in order to heal one must experience pain and suffering. Don't numb yourself to your trials and difficulties. It does not happen overnight. Lives don't get messed up in a day, and it takes time, perseverance and patience to rebuild your life, but it can be done.

There are common residual psychological issues and "coping mechanisms" after a survivor has managed to leave. I suffered from a total loss of self-confidence and self-esteem. I was not alone; my children suffered the exact same loss and depression just as I had.

With every step and every decision I now had to make I felt lost; the struggles I was facing were a constant uphill battle. I had to learn to make choices and live with the consequences, and sometimes I lost but I kept on trying. Quitting wasn't an option. Don't be afraid to fail. The important thing to remember is: DON'T GIVE UP.

Looking into your past and present, identifying yourself appears to be the biggest hurdle at this point. To remove the walls that we have put up to protect us from being hurt, we must first realize that the wall is not built of brick. The bricks are merely used in a descriptive sense; however, they are every bit as strong as an actual brick wall. For example: the Berlin Wall and the wall I have built up are both very real, and both have come down.

This has been put up around our hearts and emotional psyche to shield from the hurts that we have experienced. They are not meant to be permanent, merely a temporary fix for protection; but once set in this direction, the brain needs to be told a new direction. Because of the destructive teardown nature of an abusive relationship, we often have been told or shown that we are worthless. Give yourself permission to move on and rediscover your self-worth. Learning to love yourself and realize that the guilt you carry around is not your burden to shoulder will help you during this time. Knowing that you are a very worthy person, knowing that you were put on this earth to be loved, and knowing that you deserve the right to love and be loved in a respectful relationship are all cornerstones to your healing. Give yourself time to go through the many stages of overcoming your circumstances and events in your life.

> Scars remind us where we've been.
> They don't have to dictate where we're going.
>
> - David Rossi from Criminal Minds 2005

Forgiveness is very important part of your journey. Truly forgiving means letting go; it's a decision you make. Forgiveness doesn't mean that you deny the other person's responsibility for hurting you, and it doesn't justify the wrong. You can forgive the person without excusing the act. Forgiveness can lessen its grip on you and help you focus on other, positive parts of your life. Forgiveness brings inner peace that helps you to move forward with your life.

Science and physics have long proven that negative matter cannot exist without positive matter. In life we can choose between the negative and the positive. There is no switch; instead, it requires work from within. So far, we have assumed and believed that our life exists from the outside, and everything we are born into exists already. In reality, everything originates from within. A human being has positive energies and negative energies – our thoughts and emotions (no matter how pleasant or unpleasant they are), electronic pulses – energy running through the most complicated, most powerful matter- the human brain. The human brain is the most evolved matter on the earth. This is where we begin to create our surroundings, our reality.

Create the NEW YOU. Here is what I want you to do. Commit your very being to get to where you want to be, and though there will be setbacks, don't quit. Fear, worry and indecision are better dealt with when you clear your mind, and calm yourself. Be in charge of your emotions, learn to be in control over your feelings, and don't let them control you. Fears and limits are often part of your imagination. I have learned in life not to be afraid to fail. Mistakes are merely a life lesson, a new experience. Worries, insecurities, and indecisiveness can be your motivators instead of holding you back; don't let it be your limitation.

IT IS POSSIBLE

Repeat this with power and conviction. Say it all the time and repeat it every day. Whenever you are faced with a new situation, say, "It's Possible, It's possible, and I am Possible."

Say that until it has manifested itself into every part of your being.

But why? Because it begins to change your belief system, with such endless possibilities awaiting for you. When you start to build and change your belief system, the possibilities are endless. I want you to start believing in your dreams. I want you to have what you wish for yourself. You have to believe in yourself, otherwise you can't do it. And finally, never let anyone tell you that you can't or won't do something. It's Possible.

The Missing Piece

90

Lila Osborne

Lila is currently an Emotional Freedom Practitioner student and building her heart centered business, designed to help people let go of their fears by realizing how language and false beliefs are holding them back. Lila teaches EFT, Word Games and how to make conscious changes in everyday life. Lila also writes blogs containing informational posts like "ptsd, No Longer Gets An Uppercase In MY Life" and "Adventures of the VayJay Brigade/Art of RECEIVING."

www.MeMeWorld.ME

✉ **LilaOsborne@rocketmail.com**

Ⓦ **lilaosborne.wordpress.com**

Ⓦ **vayjaybrigade.wordpress.com**

CHAPTER 13

WHY AM I EVEN HERE?

By Lila Osborne

Who AM I? I've lived over half a century on this earth and I could never figure out why everything around me felt so wrong.

My "wake up" call came at 2 AM on January 17, 2011. It felt like a lightning bolt hit my heart and sent two surges of blood to my brain so hard and fast I thought my head would explode from the pressure. I slipped out of the bed I shared with my husband of over 33 years and quietly staggered to the guest room to try to process what had just happened and recover... or maybe just die.

For the next two days I remained in bed. I couldn't eat, drink or read. Even the birds chirping outside the window would intensify the pain. Sleeping was intermittent and the pain wouldn't let up.

I didn't tell my husband what was happening; he was on medical disability after suffering injuries he sustained saving lives and I knew he would call 911. I told him to just leave me alone, that I had the flu.

Instinctively, I knew if it wasn't my death, it was a gift. For two days all I could do was think about how the past 52 years of my life weren't about me at all; it was about everyone else. Who was I?

The previous July my husband had a "miracle" surgery that left him virtually pain free after 12 years of chronic pain on his entire right side. The pain that ruled our lives; the pain that became my prison sentence. I remember telling him so many times over the years that thoughts are things; he never listened, it was so obvious to me that the pain he suffered was his choice.

Shortly after his miracle, I began a quest of self-discovery learning how we could live a simple life and get out of debt – the debt he created. I

92

learned about the Emotional Freedom Technique during the EFT World Summit of 2010. This was my magic pill. Tapping gave me the strength to pull myself out of a deep dark pit while dragging him behind. I knew there was a reason for my life, but I was struggling to stay positive. I was learning to rise above his angry, blaming, misogynistic, judgmental CRAP. Eventually I got off the drugs (antidepressants and sleeping pills).

I was tired of not having a voice. I was exhausted from waking up in a panic almost every night and fearing the future. I think my heart was telling me I was worth so much more than he had led me to believe. I believed my life meant nothing to him as my quest for happiness had been met with constant resistance. When I reminded him that the angry words he cast out into the world in general were like arrows hitting my heart, he didn't change them. His specialty was emergency cardiology, except he had no feeling for MY heart. I was exhausted, beat up and consumed in a world of confusion.

It wasn't just my marriage that didn't serve me; it was the same confusion I felt growing up feeling abandoned. This, I now realize, was also a gift. I was born in my parents' storm; I was assigned to carry my family's anger. All my life I sat on the sidelines and just watched the chaos, watched the patterns perpetuate themselves and be handed down for generations, all the while never having the ability to stop or change it. I believed I was powerless, useless; I had no voice. I never felt the freedom to just play. If I would have known words like "Highly Sensitive" and known about being a sponge to everyone's emotions, maybe life would have made more sense.

At 18 I married Prince Charming, thinking he would be the support I needed. Instead, I allowed myself to become financially dependent on him and hide in his craziness. I grew up with a disturbed male getting all the attention; it was a vibrational match for me. Only the disturbed male I married was smart, talented, could always make me laugh, and I knew I could help him shine. I kept believing that one day he would believe in me. Today, I realize it was so much easier to use him as a shield. I gave up my soul rather than be me.

After my "wake up" call, I wanted my heart to stop and end it all, but I knew if I died the patterns in my family would continue. Who would stop the CRAP for my grandkids? I know what beliefs I passed on to my kids; they deserved a better example of what a parent should be. If I survived, I had time to change that. I always felt so different and weak; after two years of searching, I understand why. I recently heard that the worst partnership is between a narcissist and an empathetic person; it could take decades to get out of it. I bought the T-shirt on that ride. It was a roller coaster, and I rode it with my eyes closed.

What kept me relatively sane? It was the songs on the radio and their messages that helped me survive the chaos I saw around me, giving me hope that one day I would be surrounded by people that felt the same way as I do – that somewhere there was someone that would respect and love me.

It's been over two years that I gave up everything holding me down, all the false beliefs and all the stuff money can buy to figure out who I AM. I always thought there was someone out there that would make me feel whole. Now I realize that the songs that soothed me and gave me hope over the years were really about bringing me back to ME. All my life I've been searching outside of myself for Unconditional Love, the love that is the silent prayer in the heart of every human soul. I finally realize that all that matters is ME. I don't need anyone to define who I AM.

Today I realize that the issues I've dealt with all my life were not about me being too sensitive; I believe "they" were too insensitive. Maybe "they" are blinded as to how their fears perpetuate the chaos in their own lives. I don't want to play that game anymore.

My story used to be homeless, jobless and broke at 52. It was a lie, that was never me; it was me transmuting.

Who AM I? I AM a Helper, I AM a Mentor, I AM a Dreamer, I AM a Sensitive Being. Today I FEEL like a Warrior...

What AM I? I AM Human and that makes ME Valuable. I AM Fallible and I like me that way.

Where AM I? For today I AM in a beautiful space in the tropics with my own balcony, a roof to watch the stars, enjoying the ocean, the breeze, the clouds and rain. I could be anywhere doing anything that

I love. There is so much to do and see; I'm ready for it all. For so long I felt like a prisoner who didn't belong anywhere, but today I KNOW I belong everywhere. I'm not afraid of the future.

When? Right Here Right Now. It's the only time we're guaranteed.

How? I have created a book of dreams. I'm writing all my ideas down and casting them into the universe to see which ones spark a flame. I KNOW that what I need will show up when I'm ready.

I see the pieces of my puzzle coming together, finding a perfect fit.

I no longer want to live in the fear and chaos that I allowed to hold me down. I have become proficient at letting go of outcomes.

Today, the theme song to my life feels like Aerosmith's *Dream On*. I am patiently flowing (most of the time), allowing my dreams to unfold. My job is to set the intention and help others let go of fears. I intend to start memes of mutual love, respect and compassion. I BELIEVE we all have a desire to freely express love for other humans but were never given the right tools. The lies we tell ourselves, the judgments on ourselves and others are based on what we have been programmed with; they are defective opinions and they can be replaced.

We all have the power to change our beliefs. All it takes is to identify the negative. Tap it out. One word. One phrase. One belief at a time. Replace them. Tap in lighter, positive, uplifting thoughts and words. Baby steps.

My desire is to see every human eradicate the lies they've been told and believe in themselves as the perfect creation they are. My quest is to help anyone that desires that change. I'm ready to play the Game of LIFE a different way. This time my eyes are wide open.

The Sanskrit meaning of Lila conjures feelings of pleasure and fun. I AM ready to claim my birthright.

Debbie McLaren

At the present time I have a full time job helping people, have volunteered as a board member for the past 4 years and just started a new business venture. I'm a singer/songwriter/musician and my future plans include a music/speaking ministry in churches. By the Grace of God I have been sober 27 years and 9 months, and I share my experience, strength and hope with others that they too may find freedom!

www.macjams.com/artist/debmac

songwritingcontest.songoftheyear.com/deborahmclaren.htm

www.debbiemclaren.organogold.com

www.oil-testimonials.com/1374066

soundcloud.com/debjmac

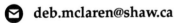 **deb.mclaren@shaw.ca**

CHAPTER 14

FOLLOW YOUR INTUITION!

By Debbie McLaren

Did you know that 1 out of every 3 female children in Canada and 1 out of every 6 male children in Canada will experience an unwanted sexual act before they reach adulthood? Almost 55,000 children and youth (0 to 17 years old) were victims of a physical or sexual assault reported in Canada in 2009.

At the tender age of 12, I was in an unfamiliar place, and a powerless lady was trying to prepare me, silently warn me somehow, but unable to protect me from what I didn't know. Intuitively, I knew she was trying to give me a message. It all happened so fast, and where was I to run? I was trapped with no way out. A person of authority, a stranger, unknown to my family, friends or community was waiting. I, a child, against an adult... I froze, became numb, tried to tell myself this couldn't be real, wasn't happening. I was in shock. He implied that if I just did what he said, it wouldn't be so bad. Then I knew. She knew; her warning, her caring enough to try to save me from this man, kept me from passing out and only God knows what would have happened then.

It's hard to explain the coping mechanism that develops at a young age, and almost in a daze, the mind goes places that the body can't. What follows is nausea, disgust, emotional and mental torture, humiliation, trauma, physical repulsion; these all filled my being. What some in this day and age might call a "mild sexual assault" or "molestation" was absolutely horrific to me. It traumatized me and blackened my whole being, my whole world, from that moment on.

As the years went by, the darkness grew inside; the shame intensified, the denial became deeper, the drinking and drugging escalated to numb the pain to forget the abuse and deny the feelings of inadequacy, low self-esteem and worthlessness always plaguing me. I felt damaged. I was violated, and thought of myself as broken and fragmented, pieces of me here and there scattered all over inside. Would I ever be whole again? Would I ever feel like myself again? Where was I to turn? I wasn't supposed to tell anyone back then or I would be in trouble. So I kept it to myself.

I thought as I grew older, this memory would have faded, disappeared. I thought I could drink it away. I seemed to forget some things when I drank; maybe if I drank more or tried some different drugs, this thing, this monster would vanish. Not so, in fact it seemed to send me on a wild ride that landed me in more situations with abusive people and the cycle continued. Abuse, drink, deny. Looking back, had I followed my intuition, it would have saved me a whole lot of abuse. So emotional from all the trauma, I couldn't clearly distinguish my gut feeling of fear, and pure unsubstantiated fear, where sometimes the fear was just a ghost trigger (by that I mean, it was something that reminded me of the abuse, but actually was nothing to fear and had no resemblance to the present situation, or flashbacks perhaps is a better description). I doubted myself more often than not, and wondered, time after time, why didn't I listen to that "inner voice" that "leave." Sometimes I was not even sure what I felt, but it wasn't good, an un-named "uh-uh-no." Some call it instinct, some call it gut feeling; I call it intuition, a sense, a feeling, an inner voice, a still small voice guiding me which way to go, what to do and what not to do. A God-given GPS of sorts, a road map of good and bad, who to be with, who not to be with, simple in theory, but when you've had years of blurred direction, it's hard to separate the truth from fiction.

I only wanted to be myself again, the fun-loving, musical entertainer who could trust people, then life would be great! The helper to hurting souls, as I myself was one. How did I get from all that to a hospital bed, angry I was still alive, after an unsuccessful attempt to end my life? I couldn't even do that right. I really didn't want to die; I just wanted the pain to stop and the abuse to end. I couldn't seem to get myself free of abusers. "How could that be?" I cried. How could that be?

The team of 5 doctors told me it was a miracle I was alive with the amount of pills I had taken, which had been in my system for over

24 hours. I should not be alive. They had no explanation other than it was a miracle. At that time I was being considered for a kidney transplant as mine were shutting down from the damage the pills had done. The main doctor sat on the edge of my bed and said they were not leaving until I told them why I tried to end my life. He said they were going to help me get better, but I had to talk, right then. He said I was worth saving. I was angry again, replying, "you don't know me, how can you say that?"

He replied, "Because I know you are worth saving."

Years of tears came pouring out and I began to tell him of the abuse. God, that team of doctors and some family and friends saved my life that day. My kidneys healed and my health was restored. I thanked God for all the physical healing; now I needed healing for all the inner wounds. The dark black clinical depression I was in, had instantly been lifted. Colors of the rainbow filled my heart and soul with joy, but I was still raw inside.

I remembered turning to God after I had read years ago that He would heal the broken hearted. Well, I certainly was that. I remembered standing in the field at home on the farm and looking to the sky and asking God for answers to my questions, guidance and help. Immediately, I was enveloped with a warm loving feeling of being totally accepted, validated, cared for, heard, understood, and loved in every cell of my being. These words I write don't adequately describe the love I felt. Human love pales in comparison, and at 14 years of age, and at that moment I needed to feel loved. So I thought I would turn to God again as I had in the past. I had lost my way, and now I wanted to be totally healed. I knew for myself, He is the go to healer!

By the Grace of God, I was 8 years sober at that time, but had to face recovery from the attempted suicide. Changes needed to be made or my doctor was not sending me home. 19 days in the hospital (and that's another story sprinkled with God's miracles!!) and I had learned a few things; now I just had to put them into practice. Once the team was satisfied I was strong enough and equipped with a recovery plan and supports in place at home, they wished me well. I thanked them over and over again for saving my life, and I was homeward bound.

As I started my new single life and attended counseling, I made the changes necessary to ensure I would not remain a target for abuse anymore. I can honestly say, God has healed these wounds, and has made me whole again! I can write this and not feel the pain I once did at the thought of these things, not cry and turn to drinking, or run and end up in all the wrong places. I share my story with women and men of all ages, nationalities, all walks of life in the hopes they too can break free from the cycle of abuse.

If you are someone that would like to stop the cycle of abuse in your life, or need healing from the abuse in your life, then I recommend you try the following:

Stop running, (internally or externally) catch your breath, and be still for a while.

Listen to that still small voice, your God-given intuition.

Then follow your intuition!

Keep a journal. Record past times you followed your intuition, and times you didn't. Compare results and feelings. Seek help and accept help; it's going to take some time to process it all. One definition I have found that fits my experiences of intuition is a "knowing" immediately, without use of conscious reasoning. I believe intuition is God-given, to guide each and every one of us. My intuition has guided me to the good and warned me of the bad. It truly is our compass to help navigate our way through this world we live in.

Angela Gower-Johnson

From childhood Angela Gower-Johnson has been gifted with the ability to tap into people's energy and thoughts. As she grew older she embraced and enhanced this gift by seeking wise counsel and ancient teachings. Her natural curiosity and desire to deal with her own life challenges has lead her on a magical journey of spiritual and personal development that has spanned three decades.

Currently her coaching and consulting practice provides a one of a kind experience with truly breakthrough results for those fortunate enough to work with her.

To receive Angela's "Tools for Change" Newsletter visit her at

www.ultimatedreamproject.com

www.empowernetwork.com/angelagj

facebook.com/angela.gowerjohnson

twitter.com/angelabear

uk.linkedin.com/pub/angela-gower-johnson/b/74/a54

CHAPTER 15

RECLAIMING THE TRUE POWER OF YOU

By Angela Gower-Johnson

For years I believed that I was unworthy, that I wasn't good enough and that I would be better off dead. Not only have I attempted suicide a couple of times, I also spent every single morning and night praying that I would get cancer. I would cry if I heard that someone died from a car accident – or anything – and wonder why that couldn't be me. My past was defining who I was, and I literally hated myself. There was not one thing about me that I liked.

Despite suffering from depression and blaming my sadness on my abusive childhood and adulthood, I was still searching for a way out. I had hope that maybe one day I would be able to experience real happiness. This desire for peace and happiness propelled me forward even in my darkest hour. Over ten years ago I made the demand of myself that if I wasn't working (as in having a job) I would make my job personal development. This may well have been the first choice I made in changing what I was into who I am now.

My happiness became a priority over everything else. I believed that if I furthered my education, read books, listened to audiotapes and watched inspirational movies then things would change. All these things did help me. But the turning point for me was to change how I viewed myself and everything I did. I remember hearing someone describe success as a choice. She said that if you started off your day with seeing the act of having woken up a success, then anything you do above and beyond that was an even greater success and it could change things. That concept was pivotal to me. I started to implement it right away. Within a couple of weeks I was able to get out of bed and start living my life. All this came from just starting with celebrating waking up in the morning.

This journey of celebrating ME actually started in the year 2000 when I was looking for new training to complete. I was spending a minimum of 4 hours a day doing spiritual energy work on top of my job and raising two children under the age of 5. I then had a vision and Knowing of Native American Indians in Lake Tahoe. I left my job to fly there, having been told that I could have a day or two to sort my head out, but if I wasn't back to work in three days I was fired. In Lake Tahoe I found a gathering of 14 people who had been "called'" (energetically) by one Native American Indian Medicine Man who wanted to teach everything he knew about healing, medicine, remote viewing, manipulating energy and manifestation. Not only was he teaching, but there were other Native Medicine People from other tribes there to learn from him and also to teach and support our group to grow quickly. I trained with these amazing people for just over ten years. I would never have had that experience had I not had my past. I wouldn't have had the drive and determination for something better!

Let me clarify that all the information I had about Lake Tahoe was information received from energy work. I had no physical knowledge or proof of this. The 13 other people that were "called" were the same. There was no website, email, phone call or friend telling us about this training. If I hadn't experienced abuse, I would never have dived deep into personal/spiritual development, and I would never have had this phenomenal experience.

The first tool I gained that helped me with letting go of my abuse was that I am responsible for my life and what I choose and what I have chosen. I was able to grasp this concept by practicing an active form of Buddhism for just over a year.

I'd like to just dive in and ask you: Are you willing to destroy and uncreate everything that doesn't allow you to acknowledge that you are the creator of your own reality? (Say YES!) This is a clearing statement: Right and wrong, good and bad, all 9, POD, POC, Shorts, Boys and Beyonds.

The second thing that freed me was looking at my abuse differently. I was gifted an Abraham-Hicks Healing audio book. In it Abraham spoke of abuse and stated that if we simply changed the meaning of abuse and how other people saw it, it would change our view on it. The example was given of looking at the abuse as having eaten too many green apples. What I was able to do is go back and create new memories of my abuse. In my mind I created a wooden shack that was dark and I sat at a table where I was forced to eat green apples. Sure it was uncomfortable. Yes, I got a tummy ache. But the judgments other people have about people that eat green apples are so much easier to receive than the judgment regarding sexual abuse. The "dirtiness" that I had carried around with me just went away. Now I was someone that ate too many green apples. This reframing of what had happened gave me so much more peace and ease.

The third thing that cleared the rest of the abuse (especially my feelings towards being a prostitute at 15) was a process I created from listening to an Access Consciousness class facilitated by Dr. Dain Heer. The process is called "Wow! I chose that! Now what do I choose?"

This is how you use this process: Find a memory from your past, preferably your childhood. Find something that was a little bit irksome. You are not looking for the most life defining moment; you are pretty much looking for the opposite of that. Something that you remember that could have been better, but it really doesn't affect you that much. Once you have that memory, allow yourself to feel into it. Now read this or say this out loud 5 times: "Wow! I choose this! Now what do I choose? Wow! I choose this! Now what do I choose? Wow! I choose this! Now what do I choose? Wow! I choose this! Now what do I choose? Wow! I choose this! Now what do I choose?"

The key to doing this process is starting out with something really small and recognizing the shift from the words. Most people will feel a difference within the first five times of running the process. Once you have cleared the energy of that one little thing, move to the next little thing and then to slightly bigger things. This process is not a judging process. I know I am asking you to acknowledge your role in this, but it is not from a place of judgment. No judging. This is about YOU getting your power back.

There is no blame or right or wrong in this process. Running this process does not mean that what happened was right. It does not mean it was OK. The thing about the Universe is that it doesn't judge. Doing this process is not going to make the other person, event or organization right or powerful. This is about YOU getting all of you back.

What this process does is take you back to a time, place or event so that you can take back any power (potency, confidence, trust) that you lost there. The Native American Medicine men I trained with taught me that such events continue to siphon off your power, as you are linked to them. Running this process for small tiny events and working your way up to the biggest events will allow you to grab back every piece of you that you have given away. You will reclaim your power and be able to function from a place of confidence and total trust in yourself!

Above, I asked you a question, and asked you to say "yes." From there I wrote out a clearing statement. This process is from *Access Consciousness*, and the clearing statement clears layers of energy (in a nutshell). You don't have to know what each word means or how it works for it to have an effect. It just does. To find out more about the clearing statement you can go to the website: http://www. theclearingstatement.com/

Here are some questions to support you with doing this process:

Will you destroy and uncreate everything that doesn't allow you to do the Wow! Process free of blame and judgment? (Say YES!) Right and wrong, good and bad, all 9, POD, POC, Shorts, Boys and Beyonds.

Will you destroy and uncreate everything that doesn't allow you to perceive, know, be and acknowledge that you are the creator of your own reality? (Say YES!) Right and wrong, good and bad, all 9, POD, POC, Shorts, Boys and Beyonds.

Using these tools, I have shared with you that I was able to go from insecure and not good enough to totally loving myself and having complete confidence and trust in me. This process also supported me having happiness 98% of the time, which is the complete opposite of how I lived most of my life! What are the possibilities here for you?

My gift to you is the Tools for Change 3 Step Program to Remove the Most Common Blocks and Limiting Beliefs. This program is over 22 hours of audio and video designed to support you in having access to all of you and your Ultimate Dream lifestyle.

Sign up for your gift at: www.ultimatedreamproject.com

Lynda Fell

Lynda Cheldelin Fell is a married mother of four and grandmother of one. Born and raised in the Pacific Northwest of the United States, Lynda and her Australian husband found themselves facing every parents' worst nightmare when their beloved 15 year-old daughter died instantly in a car accident in 2009. Lynda is the author of "A Stroke of Love," a blog that offers grief validation, bits of wisdom, and hope. Lynda and her husband reside in Ferndale, Washington, where they are surrounded by family.

Phone: 360-510-8590

www.goodgriefww.com

www.astrokeoflove.blogspot.com

✉ **lynda@goodgriefww.com**

f **facebook.com/lynda.cheldelin.fell**

CHAPTER 16

DON'T CHASE THE SUNSET: FIVE STEPS TO FINDING THE SUNRISE IN THE DARKNESS OF GRIEF

By Lynda Fell

Grief, one of the darkest journeys known to mankind, is a powerful, complex response to profound loss. It touches every culture, ethnicity, and religion in the world. It is a universal language, yet remains hard to express in spoken words. Grief can overpower every facet of one's life, yet is an intertwined part of life itself.

On August 5, 2009, I came face to face with the black depths of grief when our third child, our 15 year-old daughter Aly, died instantly in a car accident while returning home from a team fieldtrip. A stellar academic student and year-round competitive swimmer, she had her sights set on reaching the Olympics when she and a handful of teammates travelled to Seattle to watch national swim champions compete in the U.S. Open. After a long day, making the last leg of their drive home late at night, their car was hit broadside at high speed. Our daughter died instantly with her horrified teammates helpless to save her.

My life became a blur of pain so deep. I remember very little of those early months. I recall only fragments, like little snapshots of time taken during flashes when life briefly came into focus. Most of the time however, I was buried deep in the dark fog of anguish from which there was no escape.

One night I had a vivid dream that offered a philosophical lesson. In this dream, I found myself frantically chasing the setting sun. I ran with a great sense of desperation, yet the sun continued to descend below the horizon just out of reach. The black night raced toward me from behind, threatening to swallow me any moment. Oh, how I was deathly afraid of that darkness for it was so terribly black and scary. But the message was clear: The sun would rise in my life once again, but not from chasing a sunset I couldn't catch. I had no choice but to turn around, face the darkness head on, and begin walking. Yes, I had to walk through the terrifying darkness of grief. Only then would I see the sunrise once again.

When one is grieving, every moment is crushing, overwhelming, and exhausting. The sadness cloaks every aspect of your life with no offer of escape. How do we not only face the grief, but then walk through it? How do we survive?

Grief has been part of mankind since the beginning. As it is with all species on earth, new life cannot spring forward without death to balance it out. But because this journey is slow and the anguish so profound, how does one find the strength to endure the ride and return from the dark abyss? By facing each moment one at a time, then using very small steps to get through them.

BABY STEP #1: GETTING OUT OF BED

In the early days of profound grief, exhaustion sets in easily prompting many to give up before the day has even begun. After all, what difference does it make whether we grieve in bed or grieve in the kitchen? At least in bed, we can pull the covers over our head in an attempt to shut out the ugly reality, right?

As it is with every substantial challenge, we always have a choice. And for those experiencing profound grief, that first choice is whether to get out of bed. Or not. Not only does the act of getting out of bed signal your brain that you survived the wretched night (staying in bed signals that the wretched night isn't yet over), but getting up allows you to be surrounded by supportive family and friends during this fragile time. Even if you go about your day in pajamas holding a big box of tissue, you've taken the first step every morning to greet your day, however painful it may be.

Not only is getting out of bed itself symbolic for hope – hope of survival, hope that the pain will eventually lessen, hope that we might figure out how to put one foot in front of the other – it also avails us to the support we desperately need. Yes, one must dig deep within to find the strength to face the fresh devastation that each morning brings, yet, with time, choosing to get out of bed offers us so many more possibilities. Staying in bed offers us nothing but delay in our effort to reassemble the pieces of our life.

BABY STEP #2: TLC

During intense grief, it can be helpful to consider yourself in an emotional Intensive Care Unit and treat accordingly. Soothing sensitive parts of your body with tenderness is an attentive way to honor your emotional pain and can go a long way toward comforting the whole self. If wearing fuzzy blue socks offers a smidgen of comfort, then wear them unabashedly. If whipped cream on your cocoa offers a morsel of pleasure, then indulge unapologetically. While these small gestures do nothing to erase the emotional heartache, they do offer a reminder that not all pleasure is forever lost.

This isn't an excuse for irresponsible or unhealthy behavior. Rather, it's an opportunity to treat our five senses to something soothing, anything that offers a perception of delight. With practice, that awareness of delight will no longer require effort, and can help to balance the sadness.

BABY STEP #3: SEE THE BEAUTY

Profound grief can appear to rob our world of all beauty. Yet the truth is, and despite our suffering, beauty continues to surround us. The birds continue to sing, flowers continue to bloom, the surf continues to ebb and flow. Reconnecting to our surroundings helps us to reintegrate back into our environment. Begin by acknowledging one small pleasantry each day. Perhaps your ears register the sound of singing birds. Or you catch the faint scent of cookies baking in a neighbor's kitchen. Or notice the sun's illumination of a nearby red rosebush. With time and gentle effort, doing so will eventually become second nature and require no effort, and offers the simple affirmation that our world truly isn't devoid of all beauty indefinitely.

BABY STEP #4: PROTECT YOUR HEALTH

After our daughter's accident I soon found myself fighting an assortment of viruses including head colds, stomach flus, sore throats and more, compounding my already frazzled emotions. It was then that I realized how far reaching the effects of grief has, that it truly touches every part of our life including our physical health.

Studies show that profound grief throws our body into "flight or fight" syndrome for months and months. This prolonged physiological response can often cause physical unbalance resulting in compromised immunity and illnesses. Thus, it becomes critical to guard our physical health. Resist the urge to seek refuge in damaging substances such as alcohol or illicit drugs. Instead, nourish your body by way of healthful eating, small amounts of light exercise such as walking with a friend, and doing your best to practice good sleep and hygiene. A stronger physical health can help anchor us in times of emotional upheaval.

BABY STEP #5: FIND AN OUTLET

In the early part of the journey, everything is painful. What used to be routine activities, such as moving about, breathing, and eating, are all now exceedingly excruciating. Finding something to distract you from the pain, occupy your mind, and soothe your senses can be tricky, but possible. Three months after our daughter's accident, my dear husband and I sought refuge in a quaint little town on a nearby island. While browsing through the boutiques with a heavy heart, I stopped to admire a basket of highly fragrant soaps. On a whim, I decided to teach myself how to make soap and soon discovered that the soothing action of stirring a pot of fragrant ingredients proved to be very therapeutic. Thus, making Tear Soap became my vent for many months.

Finding a creative outlet for sorrow can lead to some lovely treasures. Taking up beading can result in beautiful gifts of jewelry. Learning to mold chocolate can be very soothing and delicious. Digging into an ignored corner of weeds can result in a beautiful memorial garden. Performing a peaceful repetitive act can soothe your physical senses and calm your mood, and can result in a new craft or a few treasured gifts made from the heart of hearts.

The five baby steps above are just that – baby steps. While they don't erase or invalidate the pain, the truth is that if you treat yourself kindly, allow yourself small measures of comfort, and find a healthy outlet for your grief, you'll feel better. And if you feel better, you'll cope better. These steps not only can help bring you comfort, but they can also offer focus and purpose, a light in the darkness, until you find the sunrise once again.

Lisa Kroeger

Lisa completed university in 2002 with an education in criminology and psychology. She has 17 years' experience in the areas of youth corrections, counseling, crisis, and family needs assessments for children and adults. Her work includes child development, transitions and addictions counseling.

Her first self-help book, *Unmask the Liar: a Journey Through a Decade of Domestic Violence and Beyond,* came out earlier this year.

First and foremost, Lisa is a dedicated wife and mom of three busy boys.

To learn more about Lisa, her cause or her other publications please visit her website:

www.lisakroeger.com

facebook.com/lisa.kroeger.10

twitter.com/unmasktheliar

CHAPTER 17

CHAMPIONS OF HOPE UNMASKED

By Lisa Kroeger

I thought God had sent him to me so that I could help save him.

I met him when I was 20 years old, a young single mother working for social services and wanting to save the world. He was 7 years my senior, polite, handsome and strong. I was academic and proper, and he was a bad boy who built big beautiful custom homes for a living.

That moment in time, 15 years ago, launched me into a decade of pain, control and isolation at the hands of a deeply disturbed man.

The bruises I could hide weren't much of a problem; it was the ones I couldn't hide that posed a problem. I suffered through a broken wrist, ribs and a broken face, which took 3 and a half months to heal. When I was out in public or attending university people would stare at me and whisper because I looked like a monster. My face was grotesque highlighted by shades of purple, yellow, blue and black. I knew what they were thinking, and they were right too!

I sustained multiple head injuries sometimes to unconsciousness. I was physically and mentally isolated from the world. He would move us repeatedly away from friends and family that got too close. We would move to isolated properties where I wouldn't know anyone and had no vehicle.

He would go on wild drug and drinking binges, which often resulted in out-of-control temper tantrums causing insurmountable property damage to my home, which should have been the one place I felt safe and secure. Instead I had constant reminders of how unsafe my home really was for my children and myself.

My abuser would blame me for his hurtful actions and constantly reinforce to me that no one else loved me and that I was lucky that he did or I would be all alone. And I believed him.

I was called vile names daily, as my learned immediate response was to slink to and barricade myself in my bedroom: my sanctuary of isolation.

Why would I stand for such behavior? I wouldn't! No one in their right mind would! But I came to realize I WASN'T IN MY RIGHT MIND!

During the 10 years I spent in this constant state of crisis, I had two children with my abuser who would continuously accuse me of being unfaithful to him. When I found out I was pregnant with the second of his two children, my response was to try and abort the baby. How I could allow another child to become a part of what my life had become? Thank God by the time I found out I was pregnant, it was too late to terminate because I was already 3 months pregnant. At that time my second son was only 6 months old and my first was 8 years old at the time.

Bit by bit I was slowly losing who I was and I didn't even notice. I became so ingrained in survival mode and trying to meet my three boys' daily needs that I was oblivious to anything else.

How could someone like me even consider such an alternative as to have an abortion? I realized later that this constant state of physical and emotional crisis I was in kept my body in a perpetual state of fight, flight or freeze. I could move from crisis at work in corrections to crisis at home seamlessly and it appeared, or rather I was emotionless all the time. I never cried or felt sympathy, and towards the end, I was apathetic and did not care. I just had to survive.

I thought I was an awesome mom for my boys. I thought my children had no idea about the abuse I was enduring (for their sake?). My experience tells me that it is impossible to protect your children or provide a stable home while engaged in a violent or abusive relationship of any kind. Our children's well-being is our sole direction and responsibility. If you are not healthy, neither are they. No one is worth jeopardizing your children for – even their own father.

How long does the victimization continue? When do MY CHOICES become the perpetuating circumstance that enabled him to abuse me?

I maintain that you cannot change an abusive person – ever. I believe that although I was a victim of domestic abuse, I was and stayed in this relationship by choice.

It was irrelevant what my abuser was doing, how he behaved or treated me. It didn't matter. What is important was that what I was doing kept me in the cycle of violence and abuse.

I was his biggest enabler. I would make excuses and minimize the events that took place. I would lie to my children as to where their dad was or why I was upset. I was in great denial and figured things would be different with every little change that took place within our lives. I was stubborn and didn't want to admit I couldn't FIX this, and I didn't want to succumb to failure.

It's not blame we should be looking at; it is more of not understanding our own actions or self-awareness. Actions created by our love and fear – LOVE (misguided) for the abuser, a sense of obligation and the love for our children. FEAR of harm, failure, and loneliness.

This combined with being in a constant state of crisis is a victim's death sentence if not realized.

While you stay fighting the impossible fight you may be missing out on finding true friendship or the love of your life. I was not providing my children the guidance or the example I wanted for them. Are you the role model you want to be for your children?

VICTIMS PERPETUATING CYCLE OF VIOLENCE AND ABUSE – UNDERSTANDING AND BREAKING YOUR OWN CYCLE

It begins by Accepting Inappropriate Behavior:

- **Mental**
- **Psychological**
- **Emotional**
- **Physical Intimidation**

The inappropriate behaviors can be seen in the abuser's temper, property damage, substance abuse, disrespectful actions or words and rudeness towards the victim.

Little or No Natural Consequences

The abuser often does not receive any natural consequences from the victim, like the issue even being addressed, a disagreement or the unacceptability of abuser's behavior.

Building Tension

Tension becomes intense, and mistrust and events become exceedingly escalated.

Major Act of Violence and Abuse

Possible police intervention. Often the system perpetuates the cycle, and the victim in sent back into the cycle of violence.

Minimizing

The victim minimizes the event or violent act. Victims often RECANT their story and do not support the charges that have been laid by the police. The victim experiences guilt and fear.

Making Excuses

Often the victim will make excuses for their abuser like he is stressed or intoxicated. The victim will also take full or partial BLAME for the incident.

Accepting Apologies

Victim accepts the abuser's apology. This is the classic "honeymoon" phase. This is when quiet and peaceful times exist. Sometimes it can last days, weeks or even a year.

Stimulated HOPE

This stimulates and creates "HOPE" in the victim for a better day or changing times. Disillusioned perspective of the victim reinforces self- isolation.

Mind and Body

The victim becomes sick in both mind and body. Feelings of lack of choice, helplessness, depression, physical illness and being in a "Constant State of Crisis" are common.

Victims require medical and mental intervention. It is this segment that goes untreated effectively and perpetuates the downward spiral of the cycle.

Carry On Like "Normal"

Victims continue their secret double life as "normal," and the victim continues to accept the ESCALATING inappropriate behavior.

Lesson/Homework: break down and understand your own perpetuating cycle so that you can make changes to your behavior. Follow up with reading *Unmask the Liar* for step by step support on how to leave with confidence and peace of mind. It also addresses putting a stop to ongoing victimization after you leave and how to never attract another abuser again.

Become the example you want for your children and others. You hold *The Missing Piece.* When you Unmask the Liar in yourself you will discover that.

You can be your own Champion of Hope!

Michelle E Harvie

My name is Michelle E Harvie, born in Edinburgh and brought up in Aberdeenshire. I am a healer/teacher in Scotland specializing in the Shaman ways, working with the medicine wheel. My teaching methods are to enable my students to reconnect with their true Being through shamanic healings, meditation and communication. Bringing truth to the surface while surrounding them with a space filled with love and support from a great source – light.

Feel free to contact me at:

✉ purity2010@hotmail.co.uk

f facebook.com/purityholistichealingcentre

CHAPTER 18

DESTINED TO HEAL

By Michelle E Harvie

From a very young age I became aware that I was different from other children. I saw things differently. It was like I saw things other children didn't. I stood out, to the point that children bullied me throughout school, being beaten and teased just for being me. They found it funny that I would believe they were going to be my friends then beat on me, teasing me for being a redhead and for looking boyish. It became clear that it would be difficult for me to make friends, but for some reason I always forgave them. I wanted to be accepted by them, but it always lead to more torture.

At home not much was different in my eyes. I had a sister that was four years younger than me, and I always felt as if she was more important in my mum's eyes. Especially since my mum had told me that her life would have been very different if she had not had me. I felt like it was my fault her life was so crap! She deserved more than this in my eyes. She had a husband that drank a lot, couldn't keep a job, and would move us about from town to town getting away from his debts. He also beat her.

I craved her love and would do anything to get it. My efforts were frowned upon and were seen as negative attention. She did not understand me. She did not know me really, just what she wanted to believe. I was HER disappointment after all!

I craved love so much that when my uncle showed me affection, I welcomed it wholeheartedly, sitting on his knee, getting cuddles and kisses, and believing him when he told me that he loved me. He even let me stay up later than my sister when he babysat, saying it was because I was special.

Then he began to come to the bathroom with me, and he would sit me on his knee. I didn't know what he was doing, but he said it was ok; it was what we did when we loved each other. I believed him. All I knew was that he would rub against me until he had made a mess, then he would wash me.

After a while I felt as if what we were doing wasn't right. I felt dirty, but it must be ok because he said so. I trusted him. Why did I feel bad inside though? As if I was being bad in some way. Why did I feel this was a dirty secret?

When I was 12 years old I got sex education at school and found out that what he was actually doing was abusing me sexually. I felt sick. How could he betray me? I trusted him! How was I going to tell my mum? Will she believe me? This was her brother!

I was devastated! I could not trust anyone. I had no real friends to confide in and my family had betrayed me. I was in a vicious circle, damned either way. I felt ashamed. I did not want to live anymore. I became suicidal from the tender age of 13 years old trying to strangle myself with my very own hands. I was unsuccessful. Life was agonizing. No one loved me. No one understood me.

I became scared to tell my mum of my abuse in case I would get a beating from my uncle; yet, I was getting a beating from my mum for wetting the bed most nights. This was all due to sexual abuse and how it affected my mind, a fear of it happening all over again. The memories of what he did, and rushing to get out of the bathroom sometimes with urine still running down my leg as I jumped off the toilet before he could walk in and lock the door. Sheer fear!

Finally, a neighbor told my mum of my toilet habits, and I finally was able to tell her about my abuse. I felt relieved that she knew. I thought this was it, that I was going to be alright now. She was going to punish him.

However, the night she confronted him, I sat in the stairwell and listened to her. When he finally admitted what he had been doing to me, she let him off because he was "family." I was devastated! He did not get punished at all. She betrayed me, and I was angry. I lost complete faith in her.

The sexual abuse did stop, however, as he was not allowed to babysit anymore. That was his punishment. I found it very difficult to forgive her for not standing by her words. I felt that she didn't take him to the police due to the shame it would bring on the family. I felt that I had brought shame on the family.

As I ventured into adulthood, the relationship with my mum deteriorated, as I never forgave her for betraying my trust. Then I realized that she too had been verbally and physically abusing me over the years, beating on me when I did not do what she asked or expected of me, trying to manipulate me into what she wanted me to be. I became very angry!

I was never good enough just for being me. Quite often I was compared to my little sister. It was like she could not see what she was doing to me on the inside. Yet I never gave up. I pulled away at times, but never gave up hope that she would eventually see what she was doing to me. Forgiving her constantly, making excuses for her behavior towards me.

Finally, at the age of 24, I ran away from home. I needed to escape, for self-preservation reasons. I married a man I had only known for 8 months thinking he was the answer to my prayers.

However, after pouring my heart out to him during yet another suicide attempt he too went on to abuse me on every level. Leading me to alcohol & drug abuse!!

My life became an existence…….

When would it end?? I wanted it to end!!

By the age of 26 I left my husband and met a new partner who provided me with faith in men again. He also provided me with two beautiful children, but soon after my depression came back and we parted ways.

By the time I was 29 I was a single parent with two children without any job prospects. We were barely surviving week to week. My depression became worse than ever, as well as my addictions! I became volatile, erratic and unreliable.

The week before my 30th birthday I decided that my children would be better off with anyone but me, and again I tried to commit suicide while they were with their father.

I nearly died that day, and I am so grateful that I didn't. I believe I was saved for a reason. I suddenly believed that day, as I ventured towards death's door, that I had a purpose.

I decided to go back to college and started to turn my life around by learning beauty therapy, complementary therapies, reiki, crystal healing and the medicine wheel.

Little did I know that this was just the true beginning of my life, as I realized that giving up was NEVER an option. All that I went through were lessons in life, and the people who were involved were my teachers. Then, through meditation and healing, I set about dealing with my fears and forgiving myself for how I reacted towards my teachers; providing them all with love enabled me to move forward. Step by step I confronted my fears and dealt with them with love, compassion and empathy for all concerned.

When we change our perspective, we change our lives from a place of anger into a place of love, harmony and balance. Without the lessons you would never become who you were always meant to be. If you have had troubles/tests put on your path and are still surviving to tell the tale, then you too are destined to heal.

HERE IS MY 30-DAY RECOVERY TIP

Recognize your traumas as your lessons.

See the people involved as your teachers.

Take action to heal yourself by starting with yourself.

1. Love yourself
2. Forgive yourself
3. Release the fear within yourself

    4. Confront your fears one by one

    5. Have compassion and empathy for all involved

Finally: Send love to all involved in each situation

After 30 days reflect on the difference concerning how you see and feel about your life as opposed to before.

Are you ready to make that change of your perspective and unveil the truth behind your lessons?

Vanessa McWilliams

Vanessa McWilliams lives in Calgary, Alberta, with her husband and two boys. At 9 years old she was diagnosed with Alopecia, an autoimmune disease that causes hair loss. Losing 80% of her hair as a child, she has made it her mission to help others through her Alopecia support groups, a thriving wig business and public speaking engagements. She inspires people to be the best they can be and feel beautiful!

(403) 464-5801

www.confidentcurls.ca

✉ **Vanessa@confidentcurls.ca**

f **facebook.com/confidentcurls**

🐦 **twitter.com/confidentcurls**

CHAPTER 19

A HAIR RAISING ADVENTURE OF LOST AND FOUND

By Vanessa McWilliams

It's surreal to hear people say they want to know about my story. They want to hear how I've fought and conquered my fears and grown into the person I am today. To be honest, I feel like I didn't have a choice. I am here to help and inspire others, and I hope as you get a small glimpse into my life and struggles, I can help inspire you as well.

1994 started out very normal. I was 9 years old, in grade 4, and I had no idea it would be the year that would change my life, forever.

It all started one day when my mom was doing my hair and found a small bald spot on my head, A couple months later she found a couple more. Concerned, she took me for my first of many doctor's appointments.

I remember sitting in a small, bright white dermatologist's office listening to the doctor talk to my mom. I remember having them poke my head and look me over. I remember hearing the word Alopecia for the first time. Alopecia, what's wrong with me?

"Alopecia is not life threatening, but there is no cure" the doctor said.

Alopecia is an autoimmune disease that causes unexplained hair loss.

I went through the rest of grade 4 trying to hide my increasing hair loss. When I couldn't hide it anymore I started wearing hats to school. Now most schools have a "No Hat" policy so this made me an easy target. It was the beginning of teasing, kids grabbing my hat off, and lots of crying as I walked home from school.

Elementary school was hard, but as I grew older and my bald head was becoming more of a reality, junior high became my next hurdle. I remember feeling scared; there were going to be new kids at this school. I would have to do it all over again, the questions, the curiosity. The first day was just as I pictured it to be, split up from my small group of friends and thrust into a teenage hell. I had tried wearing a wig when I was a little younger, but it was too "old" looking and was painfully obvious, so I decided to go on with my hat. Teasing was an everyday occurrence, which was becoming increasingly hard and really weighed down my self-confidence. One day I remember being out on a field trip with our class. I was with a friend and as we walked past a group of kids, one of them grabbed my hat off my head. As I stood there embarrassed, my friend yelled to give it back. Everyone stood in shock as the teacher scolded the boy and grabbed my hat back. I cried on the bus ride home. I cried as I walked in my front door and ran up to my room. That day I had enough. Why was this happening to me? Why were people so mean? Stares, comments, names? Why, why WHY?!

That day as I lay on my bed sobbing, I thought about taking a bottle of painkillers and just letting go. I was hurting so bad inside; I was so embarrassed to look the way I did. I am a bald girl! Hair was so important; hair defined beauty, and I looked like a boy without my hair! I was empty and I was beat down enough that I felt like the only way out was to die.

By the grace of god I was too scared to do it.

I moved into senior high with an "I don't care" attitude. I hung out with friends that were no good to be around. I physically and mentally hurt myself; I just didn't care anymore. Why should I? Drugs were an easy means to numb all the pain and the hurt that I had buried inside me. It was just easier to say "I don't care."

After a very long, very tumultuous two years I was given an ultimatum: smarten up or leave my house; my parents had enough of me and my careless behavior. They knew I had to hit rock bottom before I would change. At first, I was so angry with my parents for turning their backs on me! How dare they, they are supposed to always support me. I tried to be strong for myself, and I walked out of my house. I stayed with friends, partied, and hit rock bottom, hard. That's when I started to realize that the real people who cared for me were ready to give up on me. The friends I was partying with, never really cared about me. My whole life was spinning out of control, and I hated myself for what I was doing to all of the good people in my life.

I asked my parents to let me come back home. I had a curfew and conditions as any optimistic parent would have. I needed to be part of my family again. I think back now and I realize that they never gave up on me at all. They were all just as lost as I was. None of us had the answers. I hurt my parents, family and friends more than I could ever know, but they never gave up on me.

High school was everything I thought it would be, torture and survival. I never graduated; I couldn't sit in a classroom and concentrate with people staring at me, or making comments, calling me names. So I dropped out, started working full time, and began to rebuild my life.

It took a very long time for me to earn my parents' trust back. This will always be something that hurts me the most. Trust is very easily lost and so hard to regain.

The last of my teenage years were kind of normal. I worked full time, rebuilt broken relationships, and started to see myself in a different light. I started wearing wigs when I was about 17; they were very life like and looked much more natural than what I previously had. The wigs helped boost my confidence; I could go out in public and not be stared at, and it felt great!

Then one day I met a cute boy. I was never very eager to date, as most boys were my friends and didn't want a bald girlfriend. This boy was different. We had been hanging out with mutual friends for over two months, and I finally asked a friend to tell him that I was bald. I remember thinking, "He is going to think I'm gross and never talk to me again." I was surprised when the opposite happened. He liked me, not for my hair (or lack of) but for me! 12 years later that man is now my husband, and we have two amazing little boys. I found someone who truly loves me unconditionally.

Over the course of my 20 years living with Alopecia, I have come to realize that no matter how hard you are struggling, no matter what card you have been dealt with in life, you can make it! Life is like a mirror; when you put negative energy out into the universe, you will get it right back. If you start to change the way you think about things, change the way you approach situations and start thinking positively, I promise that everything becomes a little easier day by day. I started thinking positively, and I truly believe that everything (good and bad) happens for a reason. To shape who we are supposed to be, and what we are supposed to become.

I took my Alopecia, and turned it from a negative in my life into a positive. I started my own wig business (Confident Curls), I run an Alopecia support group, and I offer to talk about my story in hopes to inspire others. I have gone through 20 years of struggling with the words "Why me?" I have hit rock bottom. I now know that Alopecia was my path, and losing my hair has shaped me into the person I am today. Without all my life experiences I would never be able to completely understand compassion, love, and understanding for others.

No matter how bad life has beaten you down, no matter any circumstance, you have the power to change the way you think and the power to push through. You can start right now, start thinking that maybe there is a reason for what's happening; think about what can come of it, what can this be teaching you? Start small and work from there. It's as easy as one foot in front of the other. Just make sure you keep moving forward, you may surprise yourself!

Just remember that life is a mirror, so start thinking positive!

I want to say "Thank you" to my parents, younger brother and all of my amazing family and friends who have stood by me through my struggles and achievements. Without you all, I wouldn't be here today. I love you.

Carrie-Ann Baron

Carrie-Ann is a Recovery & Wellness Life Coach who takes her clients on a journey of releasing the weight of the world, rediscovering who they are, and awakening to the possibilities. She is a Certified Trainer of the Fearless Living Institute and a Recovery Peer Specialist. Carrie-Ann is a recurring guest on Stress-Less Radio, Contributor to Soulwoman eMagazine and an active champion for the Freedom & Empowerment Campaign. She is also an Ironman triathlete (swim/bike/run).

Phone: 403 975 2597

www.solvocoaching.ca

solvocoaching.wordpress.com

✉ carrieann@solvocoaching.ca

f facebook.com/SolvoCoaching

🐦 twitter.com/SolvoCoaching

in ca.linkedin.com/pub/carrie-ann-baron/4a/951/6a5/

CHAPTER 20

HOW ATTACHED ARE YOU TO YOUR UTERUS?

By Carrie-Ann Baron

I was a late bloomer, if you know what I mean. It was the middle of grade 9 when it started. Mornings were the worst. I would wake up in a very groggy state with the all-too-familiar impending sense of doom.

This was my life everyday from age 15 to 36.

AG 15

Menstrual cycle started, my numbness/shaking of hand started. I was told that I was just stressed and over-sensitive.

AGE 25

I was diagnosed with benign nocturnal Epilepsy and started taking an anti-seizure medication called Valproic Acid.

AGE 33

I was episode-free for 5 years and went off the Valproic Acid. Within 6 weeks, I was diagnosed with Erythema Nodosum (EN; a swelling of the soft tissue underneath the skin on my shins, PAINFUL).

AGE 34

Between the edema, Erythema Nodosum, intense PMS, prolonged cycles, anemia due to blood loss, physical exhaustion, mental strains, financial difficulties, mobility issues AND my insistence on keeping it all to myself and not asking for help, it was all I could do to get out of bed and go to work.

During this time my body was telling me to rest and let the world rush by while I stayed still. I took the time to heal my soul, my connection to god, the universe and my humanity. I explored many avenues – holistic, metaphysical, yoga, meditation, chakra alignment, and neuro-linguistic programming (NLP). I found tools from each practice that provided me the ability to truly distinguish what is, what was, and what remains. This started my adventure in discovering the difference between "good stress" and "bad stress"; "good fatigue" from "bad fatigue." I learned to live and enjoy life within the limitations that my body was in.

AGE 35

Turns out that I never had epilepsy; the neurologist I saw indicated that "given the information they had at the time and the results of your tests, the diagnosis is not surprising. The tests did conclusively show that you have abnormal brain wave patterns." Well, that didn't make me feel any better, and ANGER set in.

They did confirm that I actually do have a panic and anxiety disorder.

I went on a journey of releasing the weight of the world. I found peace in accepting what is – being content with what I had at that moment.

The doctor felt that with everything else under control, we could now ascertain the true cause of the heavy bleeding. Understanding that hormones (birth control) are a trigger for EN, using pills to regulate my period was not an option. He sent me to a gynecologist and her first suggestion was, yep, you guessed it, birth control. I tried to explain to her that it wasn't an option, but she insisted. I took the package and took them for 5 days. Within those 5 days, my manic depression returned, my anxiety hit an all time high, my emotions were all over the map and my EN/edema returned. The pain was back, and I was ANGRY.

So, back to the doctor's office I went. I was a total basket case, crying and screaming and telling them that they aren't helping me and only making things worse. I knew they were, but darn it, it sure didn't feel that way. I went off the pill immediately, and went to a new gynecologist just a few doors down. I told my story (again) to another doctor. This one was different. She sent me for an ultrasound. A few weeks later, the results came back – fibroid cysts were growing inside my uterus. I returned in 3 months for a second ultrasound to determine the speed in which the cysts were growing.

My uterus had grown from 12cm to 18cm in under 6 months. I recall the resident family doctor telling me that the cysts had grown dramatically since the last ultrasound. I asked what that means. He responded with "How attached are you to your uterus?" I was floored and burst out crying and yelled, "I DON'T KNOW!" And then, quietly whispering said, "I have never thought about it before."

He quickly left the room and brought in a nurse to console me. When I had finally gained my composure, I left the doctor's office and returned to my apartment.

I was filled with ANGER at the world; everything seemed so unfair. I really did try to be a good person. When I got home, someone was parked the wrong way and using the wrong door to move into the building. HOW DARE THEY! HOW COME THEY CAN, BUT I COULDN'T? WHY IS THE WORLD SO UNFAIR?

I stormed up to the landlord's apartment (right next to me) and expressed my frustration. He looked at me, aware my condition stems from more than just a truck being parked in the wrong place. He asked me what happened. I told him that life is just so unfair. He nodded and gave me a hug, walked me to my door and told me to lie down and rest. What seemed like only a few moments and at the same time, eons later, there was a knock at my door, it was my landlord's wife.

I wrote a poem about what happened next.

> Alone in my home
> focusing on the task at hand
> A knock on the door
> who could it be?
>
> Looking through the peep hole
> I see my neighbor
> she has two cups of hot apple cider
> and some treats on a tray

I open the door
Understanding why she came over

We sit in the living room
Sipping on apple cider
She listens to me rant
She listens while I try to make sense of it all

She is here for support and
She even laughed at my attempts at humor
She said it is okay to be mad,
It is okay to be sad
It is even okay to be calm.

Knowledge, understanding and wisdom are the keys
The unexpected kindness of others
is what keeps the spirit of hope, the spirit of peace
and the spirit of love alive.

After she left, I sat with it all – the injustice, the anger, the understanding, and appreciation of the momentum of this health discovery.

A couple days later, I received a phone call from the gynecologist's office. It was time to discuss options. She said there were only 3 options to consider, but the first two were just temporary fixes and the third option was a complete hysterectomy.

Based on my reaction at the doctor's office, I was sure this would be a tough decision for me. Then my gynecologist said this, "The surgery is inevitable, so you can continue to go through this every month for the next 20-30 years; or you can have it now, heal really fast (because you are young) and enjoy the rest of your life being healthy and pain-free. " An answer to my prayers? A way for all the exhaustion and fatigue to finally go away and no reason to use my coping strategies anymore? Without a blink of an eye I said, "LET'S DO THIS. I want my life back. I want to feel healthy when I wake up. I want to be physically active again."

We talked about giving up my fertility. Could I conceive if I didn't have the surgery? She candidly said "yes," but it most likely would be a difficult pregnancy given all the conditions I have. She told me to go home and think about it, make sure that I am completely ok with this aspect of it. After all, I was 35, single and had no kids. It was possible that I could meet someone and that we would want a baby. So much to think about, to consider.

Over the next week or so, I contemplated my future. What was in store for me if I did? What would happen if I didn't? Am I being selfish by having the surgery? A lot of feelings surfaced. In the end, I realized that the universe was providing me an opportunity to repair my health and be restored to my authentic self. It would be selfish if I didn't take this step.

Surgery was scheduled for April 7, 2008. This was the day I said, "yes" to living and "goodbye" to waiting. Was my decision selfish? No. I understood it was Self-LOVE. It was the missing piece – having an opportunity to reclaim and rebuild my life, awakening to all the possibilities available to me. After this realization while standing in my truth, it was quite easy to accept my decision and ENJOY my life rather than be waiting for just one normal day.

Finding love with myself is so much more powerful than looking for love from the outside, from someone else. Seeking love and knowing love are very different journeys.

Stacy Roorda

Stacy lives in the Pacific Northwest with three kids, many pets and an amazing husband. She has lived a life of adventure, and is now happy to be a Domestic Diva. Stacy is surrounded by loving supportive family and friends. She loves doing bible study and helping out at church. But most of all, she loves meeting other people with heart-wrenching stories. There is strength in numbers, and together we can help each other heal.

Stacy Roorda can be reached at:

📧 sunnybynature@comcast.net

📧 stacyroorda@gmail.com

❶ facebook.com/pregnantwithcancer

CHAPTER 21

PREGNANT WITH CANCER

By Stacy Roorda

"I shouldn't be here, I don't have time for this," kept running through my mind as I sat in my little cubicle in a drab hospital gown waiting for them to come get me for my needle biopsy. I went from a normal busy mom to that of a patient. I was no longer in control. I had to push my hectic schedule aside, and it felt scary. The fact that I had to drive 30 minutes and find someone to watch my two small daughters didn't matter. The techs were busy going about their daily jobs, deciding what to eat for lunch and chatting as they walked up and down the hall. They were about to insert a large needle into my breast and extract part of the mass they discovered to see if it was positive for cancer. Why on earth couldn't they just suck the whole thing out?

As I sat there I thought of our two daughters who were busy playing at home with their aunt. Hannah was our fiery redheaded 4-year-old and quite the leader. She was busy and bossy but lots of fun to play with. Zoe, our little toe-head with large bright blue loving eyes, was calmer and not nearly as independent and fearless as her older sister. "Come on Zoe" was yelled a hundred times a day at our house. Little did they know their lives would quickly turn upside-down. Their mommy would soon be gone a whole lot more for treatments that would make her very sick and bald.

I was called back, and as I lay on the table staring at the screen I realized it was completely foreign to me – the dark images on the monitor, the language the techs were using, the smells of hand sanitizer. These would all become quite familiar over the next few months. All I wanted to do was get my clothes back on and get back to my life.

I got the call the day before Thanksgiving that the biopsy came back positive for breast cancer. It was at least stage 3 with lymph nodes involved. I needed to start treatment right away. I was overwhelmed with the flurry of activity and the sheer amount of time this cancer was going to take up and, worse yet, take me away from our daughters. I was an independent fierce fighter from the beginning, so off I went scheduling, managing and organizing our new life around many appointments.

Through more tests we learned the cancer was estrogen positive, meaning its food source was estrogen, and it was aggressive. It was a tough cancer, but I was tougher. I was a firm believer in Jesus and happily involved in our church. I'd never really had my faith seriously tested, but I knew I loved the Lord and He loved me. I knew with God's help, my husband Matt, and our group of family and friends, I could beat this.

I was to have one more scan on Monday then start chemotherapy. The Friday before, my phone rang and it was my doctor. "Stacy is there a chance you could be pregnant?" I hesitated and said, "Well I suppose so." He quietly replied, "I just got back your blood labs and shows the HCG pregnancy hormone. You need to come in now and if your hormone level has risen then we can't do the PET scan on Monday." For the first time in the last few weeks of this crazy cancer journey I froze and didn't know what to think. What did this mean? Could I really be having another child at 37 years old? What do we do? Those were just a few of the questions that filled my brain as I sat in the lab while they drew blood. As I walked to my car I asked, "God what does this mean?" I immediately got an image of a harness that race car drivers wear. The feeling was instant. "Sit down and buckle up. It's going to be a rough road but you'll be fine." I grabbed onto that thought and never let go.

The results came back; I was pregnant. I went to Seattle for consultation since my doctors didn't know what to do with me. Matt and I sat there as the new doctor said I needed to terminate. He said he didn't even know if he could save me now since the cancer was in my lymph nodes and aggressive. Not only was the cancer stage 3 or 4 but also estrogen positive, feeding on the one thing my body was going to start producing a whole lot more of. Finally, he stopped and said, "I want to know, without judging you, why you won't terminate?"

I looked straight at him and said, "I wouldn't give up my other two children, I'm not giving up this one, so you need to figure out a plan B." He was caught completely off-guard but finally said, "OK, we can use adriamycin/Cytoxan on pregnant women. It's not really used anymore, but it's our only choice." He walked out with his team of doctors and students.

Matt and I just sat there. We were newly pregnant, fighting cancer and in total shock. Just as I was beginning to wonder if this was the right choice, one of the students snuck back into our room. She quietly said, "I'm a Christian too, and I want you to know that it's a baby, not a fetus, and you're making the right choice. I'll be praying for you." Both Matt and I burst out sobbing. We hugged and thanked her. It was exactly what I needed to hear at that moment. To us this wasn't a decision. This was our child.

5 rounds of chemo later, I was finally scheduled for a lumpectomy. The tumor had shrunk small enough for them to take it out. I was 32 weeks pregnant so if the surgery threw me into labor then our third daughter would have a fighting chance.

The night before surgery my back was hurting. When we checked into the hospital the next morning I was in terrible pain. I couldn't find any position that was comfortable. I asked the nurse for something for the pain. She called the doctor who immediately scheduled an MRI. I asked why when it was probably just a pinched nerve. She replied, "Stacy you've not once complained through all of this. When you say you're in pain after all you've been through, I'm going to order a scan."

The surgery proceeded and all went well. Thankfully our baby girl did just fine. My husband and I breathed a sigh of relief. I had to have radiation for 2 months but then I was done. I was reaching the finish line and could put this dumb cancer behind me and join the ranks of survivors. Then the results of the MRI came back. The doctor came in and said, "The cancer has spread to your spine which means it could have spread to the baby. We need to deliver her now." I was totally shocked. I thought back to the image of the seat belt and had a very serious conversation with God. "How could this be?

What does it mean? I don't remember signing up for this part. I've done everything you've asked, and I've trusted you. You brought us through this journey. We've been lifted up in prayer by loved ones and strangers around the world. How could this be?"

Once again, I got the feeling God was indeed there and would bring me through it. Everything happens for a reason. I had no idea the blessings that would come out of this for not only me but also many others. He gave me a peace that surpassed all understanding. I was strong, but Jesus was stronger. All I had to do was keep praying, lean on and trust Him. He would take care of the rest and He has.

24 hours later I was moved from the surgery floor to labor and delivery. They broke my water and Jazmine Stacy Roorda was born. She was only 3.5 pounds, but perfect in every way. She's a very charismatic girl with strawberry blond hair and a hugely infectious smile. She's a miracle and is here to make this world a better place. I will have cancer the rest of my life, but I'm surrounded by love on all sides and I have the promise of heaven to look forward to. Life still has ups and downs, but I'm thankful for every day I have.

The lesson I would like to pass on is to not judge people and pay more attention to your own life and your choices than to theirs. Until you walk a day in their shoes, you really don't know what decision you would truly make. Learn to forgive yourself and others. Have a relationship with Jesus, His love is unconditional. He will guide you and He will make your paths straight. All you have to do is ask Him into your life and spend time every day praying and asking for His guidance. Love yourself, heal your heart and trust your inner voice. It's God's way of directing you through this crazy wonderful life.

Mary Jo Gran

Mary Jo Gran was born in Bellingham, Washington, where she still lives with her husband, Mike. She has two sons and four granddaughters.

She has owned and operated her own business for over 29 years. It has become her quest in life to educate others in drowning prevention after the loss of her son Jim. In 2010 she was responsible for the first life vest loaner kiosk to be implemented at Larrabee State Park.

A legacy for her son.

You can contact Mary Jo at:

✉ Jimslegacy05@gmail.com

🅕 facebook.com/Mary Jo Gran

CHAPTER 22

JIM'S LEGACY

By Mary Jo Gran

"One day a son asked his father, 'Why is it always the best people who die?' The father answered, 'Son if you were in a meadow which flower do you pick?' The worst ones or the best?'"

On March 11, 2001, my son Jim Robinson and his friend Braden embarked on a kayaking trip. They were 20 years old and had never kayaked before. They borrowed two kayaks from a friend and drove to the boat launch at Cove Road in Bellingham, Washington. Jim parked the truck and they unloaded their kayaks. I can only imagine how excited they must have been, because Jim left his cell phone as well as his camera in his truck. Witnesses say they saw the boys and waved to them around 3:00 PM. After that no one knows exactly what happened. What we do know is the weather changed around 5:00 PM. It started to rain and the winds picked up.

When 10:00 PM came around and Jim had not returned the borrowed kayaks, his friend Ryan called our house to see if he and Braden were there. My husband, Mike, asked him if Jim's truck was still at the boat launch. When Ryan told him it was, he knew immediately something was wrong. He called the Sheriff and reported the two boys missing then drove down to the launch where he met Search and Rescue, the Sheriff, and Braden's parents. Search and Rescue helicopters searched the waters with infrared lights looking for body heat and they had scent dogs search the area as well.

I will always wonder where Mike found the strength to stand alone knowing Jim was missing. He didn't call anyone during the night and as every minute passed his heart sank. You see, I had left the day before to go to California because my dad's wife had passed away unexpectedly.

At 6:00 AM the next morning I got a phone call that would change my life forever. Mike told me that Jim had gone on a kayaking trip in Bellingham Bay on Sunday and had not returned by evening. He then told me they had been searching for 8 hours at that point and hadn't found them.

I will never be able to put into words how I felt at that very moment. The day before at approximately 5:00 PM I had an overwhelming feeling of dread. My brother Jim and I were in California to be with our dad at the time. A very strange feeling came over me. I couldn't tell if I was sick or what. I had never felt so disconnected from the world as I did at that moment. I just knew something was wrong. Today, I know it was Jim coming to say goodbye to me. The link and bond we had was now broken.

After I hung up the phone I felt numb, I was shaking and could hardly think straight. My brother arranged for us to get a flight back home. It took us 11 hours to get back to Bellingham. My twin brother met me and we were driven to the fire hall where all our family and friends were waiting. I remember walking into the hall and I kept walking until I came to a back room. I walked up to Braden's mom, Vicki, and reached out to her saying "I'm Mary Jo." She stood up and we hugged. We had never seen each other before that time. It was as if Jim led me to her. That very moment we found a bond that only we can share. She has been there for me, and I for her, ever since then.

I can hardly remember clearly, but the nights and days were all the same. I couldn't sleep as I heard the wind and rain beat onto our house. All I could think of was Jim out in the cold needing to be found. I felt helpless and hopeless. I was his Mom and I needed to help him.

By Wednesday the search was called off. The weather was horrible and I think they knew it would now be a recovery effort. We, as a family, wouldn't give up. We called Whitewater Engineering Helicopter Service and hired them to search the following day (I want to add that they refused any money for their efforts). We met them at the airport and were surprised when one of the pilot's friends was there with his helicopter as well. They took us up and showed us how they would do a grid search and then dropped a few people off at a time to search beaches on the islands. To describe how it felt flying above the waters looking for my son's body is impossible. It was one of the worst things ever.

The weather here in the Pacific Northwest in March can be stormy, and that it was. It hadn't let up in days. I think I knew by then that Jim and Braden weren't going to be found alive, but I couldn't give up hope. Friends helped us by setting up contact people and places, so we all could know where one person had searched and so on. Each night we pulled out the map and planned the next day's search. I remember begging God to tell me where Jim was. If he was dead please let us find him. I gave birth to him, raised him and felt I should be able to lay him to rest.

After six weeks of searching the beaches by foot, helicopter and boat, I stood there crying and screaming on the beach. I felt at that moment I was losing control. I couldn't take it anymore. I was haunted by images of Jim dying and the two boys trying desperately to help each other only to die in the effort. All of a sudden I knew it was time to let go and let God. I had the choice to continue to walk the shores looking for my son or to accept he was with God and he was safe. I chose to let go. A peace came over me. I won't say things were better after that, but I had a different mission now.

I knew I needed to make Jim's disappearance count.

I wrote letters to our Congressman, the Mayor, and the Washington State drowning prevention group to see about implementing a life jacket loaner program. This sounded simple, but it took years of rejection and determination to get anywhere. Finally, people who I had gotten to know who had some influence began to pay attention and encouraged me not to give up.

I wrote a proposal on how it could be possible to build a kiosk at the boat launch site on Cove Road with a supply of life jackets that people could borrow. There always seemed to be a reason why it couldn't be done, but I persisted and after 10 years of efforts the kiosk was approved. The Parks Department put it up. It was supplied and ready on the 10-year anniversary of the day Jim and Braden went missing. On that day I surprised Vicki by driving her there, having her close her eyes until I pulled up in front of the first life jacket loaner program kiosk in our area. She was so happy, and we both felt that Jim and Braden were there celebrating this big event with us. It's a great comfort to know that this small effort in their memory could save other lives by providing a life jacket for someone to use who might not have one. If just one life is saved, I know our boys didn't die in vain.

Vicki and I meet every year on March 11 and bring beautiful flowers to place in the water where Jim and Braden were last seen. We also celebrate each of their birthdays with our own special little ceremony.

My son Jim's body will always be missing, but the love and memories I have for him will live on forever.

Delisa Renideo

Delisa Renideo is the co-founder of Yes To Life. She believes we are designed to be slim and healthy and that when we provide what our body needs, we will return to our optimal health and weight. Delisa is a specialist in plant-based nutrition and helps people reverse diabetes and say YES! to their lives. Delisa loves living in Alaska and providing support and mentoring to others all over the world.

www.YesToLife.biz

✉ **delisa@yestolife.biz**

f **facebook.com/YesToLifeDiet**

CHAPTER 23

SAY YES! TO LIFE

By Delisa Renideo

I sat in the ophthalmologist's office with knife-like pain shooting through my left eye. I waited for the doctor to say something reassuring. Certainly he would tell me it would be all right. He was a doctor, after all! He could fix anything.

Instead, he told me, "You've got a forest fire raging in your eye. We don't know what causes it, and we have no cure for it. But I can give you some powerful steroid drugs to bring the inflammation down."

That didn't sound very encouraging, but then it got worse. "Iritis is chronic. It will come back, and every time it comes back, it will get worse. You'll probably lose your vision."

Had I heard him right? He was telling me I was going to go blind!

I was 20 years old. How could this be? I had a whole life to live. How would I handle being blind?

I immediately began looking at everything around me with more attention and intensity than I'd ever looked at anything before. I tried to memorize the sight of the alpenglow on the mountains, the fields of wild flowers, and of course, the people I loved.

The iritis subsided after a few months. But less than a year later, I had shooting pains in my hip. Arthritis. Some days I couldn't get out of bed without help, and walking was a struggle. I took powerful drugs to control the pain. Sometimes it worked.

At 25, burning pain in my stomach and bloody, mucousy stools turned out to be more inflammation – gastritis and ulcerative colitis. More doctors, more tests, and more medications to control the symptoms. And always the fear of going blind.

My 26th birthday was one of the lowest points of my life. What had happened to me? What kind of life was this? And what kind of future did I have to look forward to? All I could see was a life of pain, and a future of being blind and crippled.

I realized the doctors couldn't help me. The best I could hope for was some relief from the symptoms, but that wasn't much consolation. It seemed that my whole body was inflamed, and I didn't know where it would break through next. I was scared, scared to be very far away from doctors, scared of going blind, scared of having a horrible life.

But there's another part to my story.

As a freshman in college, I was a few pounds heavier than I wanted to be, so I started dieting. And like many women, my entire focus was on losing weight, not thinking about how healthy my diet was. So I made lots of really dumb (but not uncommon) decisions about what I ate, with no idea in the world that I was causing the inflammation that was ruining my life.

Not long after my miserable 26th birthday, I had one of those "out of the blue" experiences. It must have been an angel that came and sat on my shoulder and whispered into my ear, "Eat for HEALTH, and let your body decide what weight it wants to be."

That may not sound very profound. In fact, it sounds patently obvious to me now. But in that moment, it was a radical departure from how I thought about myself.

My attitude about my body was anything but loving. In fact, I had a punitive attitude toward myself for not having the ideal body. Specifically, I hated my legs. I'd been teased by my family that I had "Aunt Ida's legs," which was no compliment, I assure you. And it was true that I didn't have the slim, shapely legs I wished I had. But no amount of dieting was going to change that fact.

So it was a huge turning point when I decided to stop trying to force my body to be a certain size and shape and, instead, to eat for health. Looking back, I recognize that this was when I first decided to love myself. It's when I finally said YES! to my life.

I had no idea if the inflammation would ever leave my body. No doctor had given me any hope of that happening. I don't know how I realized that my food choices had anything to do with it. No doctor had ever asked me what I ate, but I did realize I needed to start being kind to myself. I needed to provide the best food I could for my beleaguered body and to trust that it would find it's own perfect weight. And I decided to be happy with whatever that turned out to be.

When I changed my diet, a miracle happened. My self-healing body responded very rapidly to my love and kindness. I didn't know much about nutrition at that time, but I used my common sense to eat as best as I could, and within days I was feeling better.

I had a couple of flare-ups over the next few years, but the doctor's prediction that I would go blind, thankfully, never came true. I've gotten healthier and healthier as I've learned more about nutrition and have lovingly eaten an increasingly healthy diet. Now, at 62 years old, I feel so blessed that the future I feared at 26 never came true. Instead, I've enjoyed an active, slim, healthy, pain-free life for almost 40 years, and every day I celebrate the ability to see the beauty around me.

I'm now committed to saying YES! to my life in every way I can, and my mission is to help others do the same.

3 STEPS TO CREATING A HEALTHY LIFE

The sad fact is that the majority of people in the Western world are overweight and suffer needlessly from preventable and reversible illnesses. Diabetes has become an epidemic. It's a horrible disease that destroys quality of life as well as shortening life, so I've chosen to focus my efforts on helping people prevent and reverse diabetes.

Our bodies are designed to be slim and healthy, and when we provide what they need, they will naturally return to health. Medical care focuses on treating symptoms, rather than supporting our natural wholeness. But the great news is, when we begin to love ourselves and provide what our bodies need, they have an incredible capacity to heal. It is now my joy to help others design healthy lives.

Although we're designed to be slim and healthy, our culture conditions us to become fat and sick, so we have to take positive action to turn that around. Hoping doesn't change our lives, taking action does. I've designed a 3-step process to get you there.

1. **Decide to say YES to your life. Love yourself, and appreciate your amazing body.**

   This step can't be skipped. We first have to make the radical commitment to love ourselves and, in love, to take great care of our bodies. Remember, this was my turning point.

   We often have a negative attitude toward our bodies. We feel critical of them, embarrassed or ashamed of them, or simply take them for granted. The first step in saying YES! to life and creating health is to love yourself. To love your body. To appreciate how it is designed to heal itself (think of all those cuts and bruises that healed themselves!)

   Take some time to think about how your body has provided you with this amazing vehicle to experience your life on this earth. Think about how it allows you to see, hear, taste, smell, and touch your world. It has taken care of you in so many ways, even when you may have forgotten to take care of it.

2. **Learn what your body needs and commit to providing it.**

   In order to have a high quality life, we need to eat high quality food. The best food for humans is whole, unprocessed plant foods: vegetables, fruits, beans, whole grains, nuts and seeds.

   Unfortunately, our culture conditions us to eat very poorly, based on highly processed foods and animal products that are high in calories and low in nutrients. This kind of diet underlies all the common diseases that plague modern society: diabetes, cardiovascular disease, cancer, arthritis, obesity, Alzheimer's disease, and more.

   However, when we adopt a high quality, nutrient-rich, plant-based diet, our amazing, self-healing body responds remarkably quickly!

After learning what our body needs, we must commit to providing it. Our body can't take itself to the grocery store – it needs us to love it enough to provide the healthiest food.

This is the action step that will translate your love into life-supporting choices that will transform your life. You can't skip this!

Also, beware of mistakenly thinking it is loving when you indulge in unhealthy food. That's not love – that's self-sabotage!

3. **Learn to trust your body and celebrate the transformation that is yours to experience.**

    If you've ignored your body's signals for a long time, it will take a little time to learn to trust it. But as you love your body, listen to it, and provide what it needs, you'll develop a deep trust in it. Your entire life will be transformed, like mine was, when I said "YES!" to my life and began eating for health.

    I wish for you the joy of living in harmony with your body, lovingly and joyfully eating the highest quality food, and returning to the slim, healthy person you were designed to be.

Linda Stewart

Linda Stewart is a Transformation Coach, Energy Practitioner and Wellbeing Consultant. She is the author of *The Little Book of Transformation* and a regular contributor to Inspired World Magazine. She is the creator and host of The Art of Transformation Global Tele-summit and creator of The Freedom Plan: Empowering and Inspiring Women to Stop Putting Your Life On Hold and Create Your Dream Life Now. Linda graduated from Westminster University in London, is a general practitioner and teacher of transformational bodywork and facilitates specialist work in the area of abuse and trauma. She is passionate about helping people transform their lives no matter what they've experienced in their past.

www.linda-Stewart.net

Skype: asklindastewart

✉ **asklindastewart@gmail.com**

f **facebook.com/theartoftransformation**

🐦 **twitter.com/asklindastewart**

in **uk.linkedin.com/in/wellbeingexpert/**

Free Gift:

Download *The Little Book of Transformation*, my gift to you at

www.Linda-Stewart.net/freegift

CHAPTER 24

YOUR POWER IS IN THE PRESENT MOMENT

By Linda Stewart

My passion for helping others transform their lives, no matter what they've experienced in the past has been fuelled by my own personal journey and the massive and ongoing transformation I've experienced in my own life.

Although my story is unimaginable to many, my message to you is that no matter what you've been through, your point of power is always in the present moment.

As a child, as far back as I can remember and throughout my teenage years right up until my 17th birthday, I experienced regular and repeated physical, emotional and sexual abuse and violence at the hands of my own father. That was life growing up in my house.

My father had a volatile temper, and my whole family lived in fear of him. There were repeated visits by the police to our house to break up the violence following complaints by the neighbors. No further action was ever taken. In those days (the 70's), it was just a "domestic" and nobody's business but the people involved.

My dear beautiful mother was diagnosed as having schizophrenia. I clearly remember the chaos, though at the time it was my 'normal'. I remember being very small, yet having to grow up and be responsible very fast. I've always wondered if my mother's "illness" (I've never really accepted it as schizophrenia) was caused by my father. I watched my father regularly beat her. I remember one time when he smashed her arm through a reinforced glass window and there was blood everywhere. I remember many times thinking he was going to kill her. But what could I do? I was very small and very scared.

COMPILED BY **KATE GARDNER**

Then one day, for reasons that were not shared with me at the time, my mum completely left the family home and moved abroad. I was just 11 years old. The violence continued. And it was shortly after my mum left that the sexual abuse started too. I was silenced by fear and couldn't tell anyone. I was too ashamed and too scared that he would kill me. This went on throughout my teens until I left at age 17 with a small case and a couple of carrier bags of possessions to start a new life for myself. Freedom.

It really didn't take very much at all to piss my dad off, and I couldn't tell you the amount of times my body was whipped with electrical cable, or his belt, or whatever was at hand and would inflict the most pain. During those times I don't remember him ever showing any emotion. Just anger. He was brutal, and I remember being shouted at to shut the hell up as I screamed from the pain and then getting whipped even harder if I dared to make a noise. My father would literally be breathing heavily and sweating giving himself a pretty good physical workout as he would punish me with his weapon of choice again and again and again. He was relentless and didn't seem to know when to stop. It didn't matter if I made my body completely lifeless. I remember at times I wanted to die.

Growing up in that household I felt invisible, worthless, unseen and unheard. I completely lost my voice. Looking back now, although every day I lived in fear, I also had an incredible spirit and unbelievable coping mechanisms as a kid, which I now call my Super Powers. I could, at will, become completely still and completely invisible and, when required, completely leave my body and have an out of body experience. Anyone who's experienced repeated childhood sexual abuse (CSA) will probably know exactly what I'm talking about.

I allowed my childhood experiences to dictate much of my adult life for many years. Although outwardly I appeared to be pretty confident and well rounded, it was all a facade. My internal world was characterized by constant stress, struggle and survival. I got very good at showing the outside world that everything was alright when actually my life was anything but. Some might view this as being strong, but inside I felt completely powerless and depressed. By day I threw myself into my work, and at night I just got numb and self-medicated using food, sex and at various times alcohol and drugs.

159

Being strong was frankly exhausting and ultimately led to a breakdown.

I found the courage to seek support, and through counseling and deep energy work, I gradually worked through everything. I experienced depression, multiple health problems and later post-traumatic stress disorder (PTSD). Recovering myself led me to complementary therapies and healing. I'd always been interested in and used them, and went on to obtain a bachelor's degree in complementary therapies and to train as a holistic practitioner, healer and now teacher.

My unfolding journey has been a gradual discovery of transformational tools, practices and processes that I have used firstly for my own healing and that have enabled me to begin to live the amazing life I am now choosing to live. I've since gone on to work with and support many women, including many courageous survivors of CSA, who benefit greatly from the therapies and transformation tools I use and share with them. And I teach, because I want as many people as possible to have these tools and to contribute to all the people that require it.

Over the years, when I wasn't battling with my demons, I was able to have some great experiences, which allowed me to get in touch with who I really am. That part of me has always been there, but mainly she was hiding. I've been on an incredible journey and have had some amazing adventures in my life like travelling solo across Thailand. Travel has been my passion, my escape and over the years I've visited numerous countries across Southeast Asia, Canada, Africa, The Caribbean and Europe.

I've always been a little bit entrepreneurial; at least that's what I've always been told. At the time I've just seen it as being in survival mode and doing whatever I've needed to do to keep a roof over my head. The survivor has always been there, but now it's my time to thrive.

I believe everything that I've experienced in my life has happened because I'm here on this earth for a bigger purpose – to help others, to show others and to be a living example that there is life beyond trauma. That your life can be better. Not just better, but more amazing than you might even imagine. I'm not going to tell you that it's easy. I know from my own personal experience that it's not. But I want to show you it's absolutely possible. And if you're not happy with what your life looks like right now, maybe now it's your time for change. What if now was your time to give yourself the life that you choose? Your life on your terms. What else is possible?

My ultimate transformation came from the realization that it was me and me alone who is responsible for my life going forward, and ever since then I've gotten into the driving seat and begun to create the life I really want to live. My life on my own terms. And that is exactly what I want for everyone, no matter what they've been through.

I'd like to share with you my 7 steps to YOUR thriving life.

1. **Take 100% responsibility for your life from this moment forward.**

   Remember, no matter what's happened in the past or what you've experienced, your point of power is ALWAYS in the present moment.

2. **Love yourself unconditionally.**

   Rebuilding your self-esteem and moving from Survivor to Thriver starts with always loving, taking care of and, being kind to yourself. This is your number one job.

3. **Get whatever support and assistance you require to release the past and move forward in your life.**

   Don't feel you are alone or that you have to do it all alone for a moment longer.

4. **Decide what YOU would like your life to look like.**

   Dare to dream and believe its possible.

5. **Commit to making your vision, your reality.**

6. **Keep taking action every day and keep moving forwards towards your dreams and goals.**

7. **Every day write down three things you are grateful for.**

Gratitude is one of the most powerful emotions and the more you appreciate what you already have in your life, the more you will attract more of what you want. Make a pact with yourself to focus on the positive.

May your strength of vision remain steadfast in your mind.

Linda was recently re-connected with her mother, who she has not seen or had contact with for over three decades. This came about miraculously via, of all things, a Facebook connection, which led to her sister, finding her mother, plus four older siblings, over 20 nephews and nieces and some great nephews and nieces. They have yet to be reunited in person but speak regularly.

Kerry Connelly

Kerry Connelly is an English-Australian author of non-fiction, self-help and tongue in cheek humor. A firm believer in the importance and understanding of those who suffer with various forms of mental health issues, her second title *Shaken: A story of emotional abuse and depression* combines personal experience with self-help sections for those who may be in need, and has been backed by writers, readers and reviewers alike. Kerry is an avid reader, a lover of all things film and television, and is also a certified education assistant.

Connect, email, find purchase links and follow Kerry via the following links:

authorkerryconnelly.wix.com/authorkc

www.amazon.com/-/e/B00CKGB060

goodreads.com/author/show/6949168.Kerry_Louise_Connelly

plus.google.com/111751769021312087963/posts?partnerid=gplp0

❶ facebook.com/authorKerryLouiseConnelly

CHAPTER 25

I MAY BEND, BUT I WILL NOT BREAK

By Kerry Connelly

When you let it get to you, there is no sunshine. I know, I've been there.

But I am not just a diagnosed major depressive. I am not just a sufferer of severe panic and anxiety disorders or a survivor of emotional abuse. I'm a woman. A writer. An educator. A lover. A hater. An advocate.

Not so long ago I was in a pretty bad place. Having suffered from anxiety attacks since childhood, it was a normal occurrence growing up to find myself locked away in the bathroom, alone and scared to death, heart racing and sweating profusely, making my peace to god, almost certain I was about to die. Now I know I was experiencing what medical professionals call the "fight or flight" response (a psychological response to what your mind may perceive as various dangers and harmful situations.) As it turns out, I was a fighter.

If it weren't for the gift of what I call my logical brain and my instinct to keep fighting, the decade known as my twenties, which at many times through overwhelming depression and emotional abuse had me fearing I may end up in the cuckoo's nest, would have been much more difficult to endure.

Alone, depressed and miserable in my twenties, not only was my job contributing to the decline of my mental health, but I was living without any family and with very few friends who cared. I continued day to day, doing the "right thing," working a full time job and taking care of my responsibilities, but I was miserable, exhausted, depressed and deep loneliness shadowed me wherever I would go. The fog of which I wandered through, led me straight to the door of an emotional abuser. A door I knocked on that opened and latched shut behind me, trapping me for months on end.

My depression grew worse under the control of my emotional abuser, which birthed the arrival of other mental health issues. Severe anxiety and panic disorder with slight OCD became the only companions to which my advanced diagnosis of major depressive disorder saw for the longest time.

Together with my abuser they would delight in playing games. "Pin the tail on the donkey" became "Pin the blame on Kerry"; "Monopoly" became "Melancholy"; and battleship just became a battle. A battle against my abuser, a battle for my own sanity against him, a battle to leave, and the continuous battle to attain a positive state of mind against the backdrop of a stormy sea.

I finally managed to leave by the grace of god and with the help of two people who I found out truly cared. Liberated from my abuser, I was still constricted by depression, panic and loneliness. Carrying my beloved pets and favorite possessions, I acknowledged my psychological companions and moved forward with my head held high.

Months after my journey through abuse ended, I started to find it hard to sleep. Memories of the behavior I was subjected to kept me in a subconscious state of fear and trepidation. One evening I started to cower with my fists held tightly on guard in front of my weeping chest. I had become nervous when for some reason I couldn't wash all the cutlery in the sink and my new partner, through concern, wanted to know what was wrong. Other times I felt ready to fight with whomever may throw me a single bone. Fortunately for me, I went hungry most of the time.

When I realized my behavior was still reflecting that of a woman in the battles of abuse, I decided to delve deeper into the topic of emotional abuse, to better understand the situation and the long-term effects that abuse had had on my mental health.

The fruits of the experience I went through as a victim of emotional abuse would begin to show themselves to me through the healing I gained through writing. *Shaken* became my first serious title, combining sections of my own experiences with self-help for sufferers of both psychological abuse and mental health issues and for their friends, family and acquaintances who may be unsure of exactly what emotional abuse and depression is and what a victim may go though.

Having deep seeded issues with ignorance and abandonment, I wanted to make those who are fortunate enough not to have been sufferers aware of what we, the abused in various forms and/or who are dealing with mental health issues, actually go through. For depression doesn't discriminate and even those with the strongest of wills may one day unknowingly find themselves in the grips of an emotional abuser. With acceptance and education, I pray no one will be "unknowing."

The book helped in my own understanding and, in turn, has placed me in a position to reach out to others by also opening an online group for sufferers of abuse and mental illness to connect and share their own experiences. It has helped me heal from the emotional abuse I endured and be able to offer support and advice to others. By using myself as an example, I am proof that you can leave an abuser. You will never be the reason that someone else abuses, no matter how many times they try to condition you into believing that you are.

Seeing my abuser as someone who is troubled himself, opened a window for me of pure and utter clarity. After all, why do bullies bully? Usually from internalizing personal trauma, hurt, loneliness and other personal issues that they themselves choose not to face, but instead project their issues, whether consciously or subconsciously and most definitely unfortunately, through abuse.

Learning to understand that I cannot control another person's actions, only my reactions to them, is a grace I try hard to ingest daily, as I know the phrase I follow, "everything happens for a reason" is as true as I am real. It must be because I'm still here.

Depression on its own, however, is a slightly different story. For the stigma and ignorance that revolves around mental illness is, unfortunately, still a prevalent issue when it really shouldn't be.

As in my case of major depressive disorder (also known as clinical or recurrent depression), when I checked emotional abuse at the door for the first (and last!) time, I realized through frustration that you can't just check depression as well. Those who live with any mental health disorder are likely to tell you the same.

While I don't wish for anyone to suffer from a mental issue, I wonder if the ignorance toward those who do suffer with depression and various mental illnesses would stop if one who is free from these things could experience it for themselves. When the universe is dealing cards, no one hopes or chooses to have a disorder and one would never speak poorly of the suffering it can cause, should they have ever experienced it themselves.

I'm not ashamed to say that depression, anxiety and panic disorders are something that I am likely to struggle with at certain points in my life, so why should I sit in shame when I can continue to educate myself, learn and grow from my experiences and not let them constantly hinder me? I am strong, that I know, just as I want others who live day to day with the deep feelings of sadness loneliness and hopelessness of depression, to know that they too are strong, for living with such a disorder is no easy task.

I am sure that at times, I may temporarily succumb to tremors and crying attacks. Yes, they will be scary and painful both emotionally and often physically. For when I am in the heart of an attack, the frustration that accompanies it can be immense. Logically, I know what is happening to me, yet my thoughts and my body choose to go off on their own tangent, trying their best to drag the logical me on down with it. This is depression. These are all parts of my disorders. I thank God for my logical brain and the gift of this knowledge. Trying to see these attacks as "getting it all out" or "purging out the hurt" to make way for the positives in your life to come, can be extremely helpful.

Somehow and quite literally, I have become an open book. And with that openness I stand tall in saying that I am not perfect, not cured or completely healed. But as a sign upon my body reminds me: "I may bend, but I will not break." Considering I created the phrase, which was not intended to signify depression, many years ago, it just goes to show that everything happens for a reason. For now it is the very personal tattoo that I share as the very fitting title for surviving anything.

Never be ashamed of what you go through, have gone through or will go through. It's okay to bend, to be sad, unsure, confused, but never let a situation break you. There is no shame in having been a victim of abuse. You were strong enough to survive it. There is no shame in living with depression. For you are strong enough to live through it.

Your life is in your hands. You can be free from emotional abuse. Depression doesn't discriminate, and ignorance will always exist.

Debra K Adams

My life perspective is framed by my experiences and education. My academic disciplines of gender, culture, and history have inspired me to break the deafening silence that weds cultural discourses, social practices, and gendered expectations of survivors of domestic violence. As a survivor of domestic violence, I have 20+years experience working in the anti-violence field. Over the years, I have provided education/trainings, as well as developed curricula on local, state, Tribal, national and international levels.

www.sisses.net
360.21.3639
debrakadamsma@gmail.com
My radio show – Debra Self Empowerment Strategies (SeS):
www.blogtalkradio.com/debra-ses
linkedin.com/in/sisses/
www.vizify.com/debra-k-adams-ma-pdv-cws
www.efactor.com/sisses
instagram.com/debrakadamsma
www.ibosocial.com/debrakadamsma
travelpod.com/members/adamsdebra
www.facebook.com/debrakadamsma
www.facebook.com/SelfEmpowermentStrategies
www.facebook.com/SurvivorsInService
@DebraKAdamsMA   @DVSurvivorUnite
@SEmpowermentS   @Debwomenspirit

CHAPTER 26

5 AS TO AUTHENTICITY

By Debra K Adams

AWARENESS

ACKNOWLEDGE

ACCEPTANCE

ADAPTATION

AUTONOMY

AUTHENTICITY

"Authenticity is the alignment of head, mouth, heart, and feet—thinking, feeling, saying, and doing the same thing— consistently."

Lance Secretan

AUTHENTICITY. WHAT IS IT? WHO NEEDS IT?

Well, if I am not mistaken, YOU do! In fact "authenticity" is what every human being is seeking.

Really, you did not know this? Haven't had much time lately for self-reflection and self-care? Welcome to the real world of adults living in the 21st century, right?

Usually when someone throws a word at me, and I don't feel as if I am getting their drift, I turn to the dictionary. Remember that "thing" that used to be a book, a big book, filled with letters and characters, defining every single word in our universe? Now it is available on the Internet -- you can AskDotcom (Ask.com), go to Google, Bing it, or even ask SIRI on your iPhone. Google is my "go-to" for serious inquiries such as this....

About 11,500,000 results and 0.65 seconds later, you will learn that the top source is the Free Merriam-Webster Dictionary. One click later, you read that authenticity is an adjective and it means, "real or genuine : not copied or false : true and accurate : made to be or look just like an original." For our use here, today, we will rely on definition 5: " true to one's own personality, spirit, or character." (Retrieved from the Internet at http://www.merriam-webster.com/dictionary/authentic on October 28, 2013.)

This is what we all seek: the opportunity to live our lives being true to our self, our own genuine sense of self. This means we can live without pretence, without putting on a false façade, without a mask. Usually we live with the fear of someone knowing who we really are and then judging us as inadequate. When we are authentic, we do NOT need anyone's approval because we have a deep understanding of our value as a human being. When we are authentic, we are our own best cheerleader, patting ourselves on the back as we accomplish our goals and tasks throughout our lifetime.

So, I ask you, will you join me on the path to authenticity? It is a journey, you know. It isn't easy or fast, and it is worth all your effort. Being "authentic" means being actually and exactly what you claim to be – the wonderful and unique YOU!

My years of experience, a compilation of personal, academic, and professional events, have taught me that many things can be self-learned. This is the method of learning, for many, that sticks with us the longest. You can see a picture, you can hear the words, but until you get the physical and practical "doing," it is just air – nothing you can feel, see, taste, touch, or hear.

This practical application of tested theories and experiments has led me to the development of "5 As to Authenticity."

The beginning A is AWARENESS: How does one gain this phenomenon? First of all, we need to take our heads out of the sand! I told you this was not going to be easy. To that end, lift your head, and open your mind, eyes, ears, and heart. Look around you. What are you seeing? The wise and wonderful Maya Angelou tells us, "When someone shows you who they are, believe them the first time." What she means is this: do not deny, justify, minimize, or excuse people's behaviors. The behaviors of people around you will speak much louder than their words. Believe what you see, what you hear, what you feel. Is your heart beating fast? Does the hair on your arm or the back of your neck stand up? Do you feel sick to your stomach? This is a clue, a cue for you. Now you must ACT accordingly on this information.

The next A is ACKNOWLEDGEMENT: This is an important action for you. You will want to tell yourself, "I just saw, felt, heard, and understood that event." Speak the words, hear the words, act on the words, and honor your intuition! Paying attention will help keep you safe. Your intuition is meant to give you warning signs of possible danger. Everyone has this inner voice of wisdom. Usually, the voice diminishes as we grow. As we age and experience life, somehow we start doubting the valuable voice inside our souls. We get into the practice of explaining away our intuitive knowledge. This is NOT healthy! Acknowledge what you know.

The third A is ACCEPTANCE: We must learn to accept the inner wisdom. Why is this step so difficult? Acceptance is surrendering, letting go. It is easier to accept than it is to fight or resist, do you agree? Brene Brown suggests to us, "Because true belonging only happens when we present our authentic, imperfect self to the world, our sense of belonging can never be greater than our level of self-acceptance." Our fear of being less than perfect, keeps us from accepting what is. The fear causes a negative impact on us as human beings. We go inward, hiding in a sense, instead of focusing our efforts on the acceptance of who we are and what we know.

This A is my favorite, ADAPTATION: Another word for adaptation is changing to meet the event or situation. I know, many of us do not like change. Over time, I have come to know that change is inevitable.

It will happen. Why not embrace it? If we have done our previous work of awareness, acknowledgement, and acceptance, adaptation becomes easier. Albert Einstein was quoted, "Our ability to change is a measure of our intelligence." Who am I, or you, to argue with a genius? As always, this adaptation phase of our journey may not be easy, simple or quick. The end result will be worth your while, I am sure!

The fifth and last A, AUTONOMY, is a word that confounds us simple humans; however, it is crucial to our success. Having autonomy gives you the freedom to make your own decisions, based on your best thinking and experience, to move forward to meet your goals in life. Autonomy is a moral independence, achieved by operating, acting, and being in this world, living up to our fullest potential. Autonomy relieves us of our fears or judgment from others. There is something to be said about the old colloquialism that says, "Don't judge me if you haven't walked in my shoes," yes? Only you can know what is best for yourself. Be confident in that and all of your decisions. Own it! Work it!

These 5 As – AWARENESS, ACKNOWLEDGMENT, ACCEPTANCE, ADAPTATION, AUTONOMY – will take you right to the heart and soul of you, that gem buried deep in your psyche. **The 5 As will assist you in reaching the pinnacle of your life's search, to AUTHENTICITY.**

I first heard of "authenticity" while reading a book written by Sarah Ban Breathnach. She says, "The authentic self is the soul made visible." Your soul is beautiful, please share it with others, stretch and reach your own authenticity. You won't ever regret it.

ACCESSING YOUR AUTHENTIC SELF EXERCISES

Write down the top 20 jobs/careers you wanted to have as a 10 years old child.

Ex: Cowboy, Secretary, Clown	

Arrange the above in order of priority; your most important identity goes on top. Any common denominators?

What is your favorite color? _____

Favorite number? _____

What was your first car you ever drove? _____

What is your dream car? _____

What is the one thing you have always wanted to do, but have not yet accomplished? _____

Name your top 5 values for a work environment, company and self.

Ex: windows	Ex: service	Ex: honesty

Place the above in priority order. Do your values align in all 3 spheres?

Name all the roles you play in your life – use more space if needed.

Ex: Parent, chauffeur, dishwasher, teacher	

Arrange these in priority order.

Write your autobiography on separate sheet of paper – use as many sheets as you need.

Write your obituary, in 150 words or less.

If you were in the ocean, paddling to stay afloat, who would throw you a life preserver? Name the top 10 people who would assist you, when in need.

Take the Myers-Briggs test or something similar (most community colleges will offer for a nominal fee).

Search the Internet for FREE resources for personality tests – for fun only!

Go to this link to find out your "True Color" (personality test):

http://medicine.tamhsc.edu/audiences/faculty-staff/resource-team/ meetings/docs/2011/jun-retreat/true-colors-test.pdf

or http://www.careerpath.com/career-tests/color-test/

Tara Tierney

Tara Tierney is an author, blogger and poet. She is currently working on a series of children's books and an autobiography. Tara is devoted to learning how to be her authentic best self and through this journey will soon be performing her first stand-up comedy routine.

Visit her blog at

www.taracle.com

CHAPTER 27

DEPENDENCE LEARNED – INDEPENDENCE GAINED

By Tara Tierney

I chose to separate from my husband, without animosity. I was learning more about myself and growing into a different person; the separation was a complete shock to him. I knew we should legally separate, but out of respect, that could wait until our teenaged daughter was finished school.

I had always lived with someone. As a teen, I left my family to live with friends, then a boyfriend, then alone with my daughter, finally with my daughter and husband. For the first time in my life, I was living on my own!

INDEPENDENCE – THE MISSING PIECE IN MY LIFE

A colleague, mentor and good friend was purchasing a house and offered to have me live in the basement suite with low rent so that I could pay off all of my bills and travel (a dream of mine). I could live there independently and for a very long time. She said she wanted me to live with her for at least 10 years, which I was more than happy with. I was content to rent for the rest of my life. I left my apartment and moved in January. We agreed that we didn't need a lease or rental agreement. We were so happy together; she would frequently comment on how happy she was that I was living in her beautiful house.

Meanwhile, my physical and mental issues were culminating in a big change. I had dislocated my knee the previous fall and, due to my morbid obesity, the pain was excruciating and lasted much longer than it should have. I was using multiple drugs for pain, as well as anti-depressants for major chronic depression. I suffer from migraines and was using birth control to minimize their impact. I realized that after over 11 years on birth control, my hormones and body were not working together properly. Through discussions with my doctor I chose to go off birth control in April. I knew this would cause my migraines to become worse than ever, but more than that, I knew my hormones would be thrown into a frenzy and I may become slightly more mentally unbalanced.

My housemate is an armchair psychologist. She is extremely interested in all aspects of the psyche, but she admittedly doesn't understand depression. With the added hormonal imbalance, I warned my girlfriend that I might be more depressed and seem more unhinged. I asked that she please not take any of my attitude, mannerisms and reactions personally, that I had to learn to handle my emotions all over again. She assured me it would not be a problem.

Within the first month she and I were having issues. She was taking most exchanges personally – at work and at home. It was very subtle at first; I thought she was learning to handle my emotions, which were admittedly pretty radical.

After my daughter had graduated around the end of May, my girlfriend came down to my place for coffee and casually asked me, "So, how long do you plan on living here?"

I was stunned. I responded that I was planning on staying the minimum 10 years that she had repeatedly told me I could, and reminded her that I was happy to rent here for the rest of my life. I asked why. My tone must have been defensive (because I was!). She replied that her adult daughter was having issues at home and might be looking for a place to live come January. I told her I had no plans to leave any time soon. From there, our relationship deteriorated.

Over the next few months, she mentioned her daughter probably needing a place to live November 1. So, taking my cue, I had to have the difficult discussion with my husband about filing for legal separation, as it was obvious I would have to move by the New Year, and it would be better to start working towards financial settlement earlier rather than later.

I am a supervisor at our shared workplace, and in August witnessed my first experience of sexual harassment. Internally it made me an emotional wreck. I felt as though I was the one harassed. I didn't understand my extreme reaction, so I discussed the entire issue with my housemate/girlfriend, as she was my mentor at work. She advised me to contact a manager and I did. I explained the situation and recommended the probationary employee be let go. My manager told me I had done everything right, and I should take care of myself emotionally. I determined my reaction was extreme disappointment as well as not being able to empathize with my employees. I knew this was true to me and was able to accept it and begin to move on.

The following week, I met with my direct Supervisor to give him the incident report and discuss options. To my surprise, I received a performance review instead, which said that I was too emotional and inconsistent as a supervisor, I was over-reacting, and it was suggested to me that I step back from the supervisor position. Also, he said in a very pointed way, if I had any issues externally that may be contributing to my emotional distress I could talk to him about it.

And there it was. Of course, by this point, I had been crying throughout the entire meeting, thinking, "I can't believe this is happening. I can't believe this is happening," further proving my instability.

My friend was avoiding me during that week and I noticed some changes at home. I was soon going on vacation and was arranging another girlfriend to come stay in my place to feed my cat. My housemate expressed that she did not want this friend to stay because she didn't know her, and therefore didn't trust her with her house. She said she would rather her daughter (!) stay in my suite. I replied that I preferred my friend; she said she would have to think about it.

She began to enter my suite when I was away to deliver my mail (we had agreed not to enter each other's living space without notice) and her dog was leaving smelly gifts on the grass in front of my door step that were not being picked up. It was obvious something had changed on her part, but I had no idea what.

I decided to try to clear the air. I began to tell her that I felt she didn't view my suite as being mine, as if I was a child living in her home.

She defensively said that it wasn't mine; it was HER house. At that point I knew the conversation would go nowhere. I wrapped it up by declaring that my friend would be staying while I was gone and that her reasoning didn't stand. It would be the same as me announcing I didn't want her best friend to stay upstairs because I didn't trust her to NOT come downstairs and mess with my stuff. She professed it was not the same at all. Conversation – over.

5 minutes later I received a text message from her; she told her daughter that I would be in my own place by November 1. I asked if that was my notice to leave, she replied that she thought that was a fair amount of time… So that was it. Heart = broken, life = complicated.

I had to ask myself what was best for me, what should I do that would be true to me? The answer (and choice) was to step back from the supervisor position at work, file for legal separation and look for a home to purchase. Accept the changes and begin to build my life anew. I put all of those choices into action and one crazy emotional month later, I was separated, owned a new apartment and was about to step back at work.

By the time the deadline rolled around, her visits into my suite to "deliver mail" became almost a daily affair. My storage had been moved out of the garage and placed on my patio. No communication, no respect. This was like a whole new form of domestic terrorism. I was not comfortable in my own home, and I had no place of respite from all other aspects of my life.

I realized that I had convinced myself I was independent when I had actually given up control. How had I been so blind? I now understood the last 2 years were the catalyst for me to find my true independence. I learned I was still depending on another person for my happiness, safety and well-being. I never actually kept my power; I was still giving it away!

I now live independently, am financially independent and in control of my own life at home and at work. It's a brave new world, and I'm so grateful to be independent.

Be true to yourself – all else will fall into place. Accept the changes and begin to build your life anew.

Conclusion

What you have read between these pages has most definitely shocked you, inspired you and left you with hope that there is life after traumatic experiences.

I hope you have enjoyed reading the amazing stories from each and every soul in this book. I hope that you take with you their inspiration, courage and strength, and include it into your life to help you move forward on days you need it most.

The one thing I enjoyed so much about placing this project together was the amazing personalities within each and every one of these women. They are so full of compassion, and, most of all, they are so full of love.

Love is always the guiding light in every dark situation, and these women completely transformed who they originally were to become the incredible souls they are today. All that started from loving themselves first. This love they had for themselves soon became evident, and it shone upon the world in amazing ways.

This was, without any doubt, worth every minute of every day that we worked on this project, because now we have brought you this amazing book!

The journey will now continue in my second project, *The Missing Piece in Business*, where we will again bring more amazing people together to become international recognized and become published authors with every intention of going for that international best seller's title.

If this appeals to you and you want to join the next project, then don't hesitate to email me at:

Kate@empoweringcoaching4women.com

For more details, check my website to enroll now at:

www.empoweringcoacing4women.com

And I will see you in the private Facebook group where we will start our journey to a new book.

I wish you success in everything you do and send you love

God bless you,

Kate Gardner

International Best Selling Author/Empowerment Coach/Video Creative Director/ TV & Radio Host and Founder of the Freedom & Empowerment Campaign

Did You Know
That Video Can Increase
Product Sales By 400%?!

Did you know that YouTube & Facebook have over 800 million active users per day?

With these huge viewing figures, how can you not afford to launch your product or business with a professional video? Or have professional introductions for your video blogs?

By using Video to launch products, you can increase your sales by 400% and open yourself up to over 16 million active viewers on the two most popular social networking sites each day!

Kate Gardner is a Creative Video Director who works with authors, business owners and video bloggers to help promote their products professionally with video trailers and professional video blog introductions. Kate Gardner has worked previously with International Best Selling Authors to promote their books, radio stations and video blogs.

Kate provides a complete done for you package which delivers a top professional service so that you can sit back and relax knowing that you are in great hands and that you will receive top quality work with zero stress.

The aim of the service is to provide you with top quality professional work so that you can look highly professional in your business and to your followers on social media.

So if you need a professional video to launch your business, product or a professional Introduction to your video blog, then check out our services today, and let's create a more professional looking video that launches your product and video blog the professional way!

Check out our website at www.succesfulvideo.com

International Best Selling Author & Empowerment Coach

The Missing Piece:
A Transformational Workshop

The Missing Piece: A Transformational Workshop travels the globe to empower women. Presented by Kate Gardner, these workshops empower and expand your mind into places you never thought possible.

Kate shares in her workshop her journey from concrete bottom to success, and gifts her students with the tools they need to feel empowered and raise their self-confidence to whole new levels. Kate also shares how you can create a huge international platform from your very own home and with a very small budget.

The Missing Piece: A Transformational Workshop will leave you with a clear direction and the tools you need to get to where you want to go. Kate will make you aware of opportunities that could lead you to success and completely change your life and open doors of opportunity that would otherwise be impossible.

If you would like to see The Missing Piece: A Transformational Workshop presented by Kate, or would like to hire Kate for speaking engagements, then please visit

www.empoweringcoaching4women.com or email direct at
info@empoweringcoaching4women.com

We hope to see you very soon!

Are You a Business Owner?

Would you like to be an internationally published author?

Then YOU can appear in the next The Missing Piece book project!

The Missing Piece in Business book project is now open for enrollment, and YOU are welcome to be a part of it. This is your chance to be published alongside successful business owners and share your wisdom with others.

Joining this project could lead to amazing connections and lifelong relationships with like-minded business owners.

This is truly an incredible opportunity to advertise your business and become INTERNATIONALLY recognized for what you do! And all for a low investment of just $450. IMAGINE THAT! You can become an internationally published author AND internationally recognized for ONLY $450! (I have paid more than that to advertise my business with posters, trust me!)

If you are interested in appearing in the next chapters of *The Missing Piece in Business*, which will be foreworded by the amazing Lisa Larter, then please visit www.empoweringcoaching4women.com.

I hope to start this journey with you in the next book and share your amazing insight with the world, which will help support other business owners. Plus, I have every intention of getting you on the Best Sellers list!

Before we went to print with this project there were ONLY 26 PLACES LEFT, so hurry before it's too late!

Here's to your success!

Kate Gardner

International Best Selling Author & Empowerment Coach
www.empoweringcoaching4women.com

Do you dream of being published?

What I enjoy the most about my business is being able to collaborate with so many different women all over the world. And the best part? When I get to help them organize their very own collaborative work — that is where my real talent lies.

Without doubt, a book is The Asset to have to increase your visibility tenfold, gain instant credibility, and increase your clientele.

So if you want to turn your dream of publishing your own anthology book into reality, get in touch with me and I'll show you how. Together we can accomplish this in 90 days, cost-free, going through everything from A to Z — including how you can actually make money right from the very start.

Sounds good?

Then email me at christine@coachingandsuccess.com

Have a wonderful and successful life!

Christine Marmoy

The End

CPSIA information can be obtained at www.ICGtesting.com
Printed in the USA
BVOW04s1846121213

338985BV00010B/71/P